RURAL SETTLEMENT AND LAND USE

Geography

Editor

PROFESSOR W. G. EAST

Professor Emeritus of Geography
in the University of London

RURAL SETTLEMENT
AND LAND USE

AN ESSAY IN LOCATION

Michael Chisholm
Reader in Geography, University of Bristol

HUTCHINSON UNIVERSITY LIBRARY
LONDON

HUTCHINSON & CO (*Publishers*) LTD
178-202 Great Portland Street, London W1

London Melbourne Sydney
Auckland Johannesburg Cape Town

First published 1962
Reprinted 1964, 1965, 1966
Second (revised) edition 1968
Reprinted 1969, 1970

Printed in Great Britain by litho on smooth wove paper
by Anchor Press, and bound by Wm. Brendon,
both of Tiptree, Essex

CONTENTS

FIGURES

TABLES

PREFACE TO THE SECOND EDITION

The task of revision has made me more than ever conscious of the plethora of material that is available and the variety of stances from which it may be viewed. I have chosen to maintain the framework and the argument in its original form even though the normative, partial equilibrium view of the world may seem a little old-fashioned. The justification is that for certain classes of problem this approach is valid and yields practical conclusions with a manageable amount of effort. Within this framework, I have sought to bring the statistics up to date, to introduce documentation where previously this was lacking and to substitute better or more recent examples. By a remarkable coincidence, the first edition appeared in the same year as Sautter published a magnificent documentation of African and European material that confirms the arguments of Chapter 4 beyond a peradventure. Since 1962, English translations of von Thünen's and Christaller's formative works have appeared but it nevertheless seems desirable to retain the outline of location thought contained in Chapters 2 and 3, though with some modifications.

Bristol, 1967

M.C.

PREFACE TO THE FIRST EDITION

To a remarkable extent, students of location problems have fastened attention upon industrial and urban matters rather than upon agricultural and rural affairs. The preponderance of the former studies undoubtedly reflects the relative importance of the manufacturing and commercial sectors of the technically more advanced countries where most students of location matters have in the past resided. Perhaps it has also seemed that the locational problems posed by city life and factory employment are more amenable than those of the countryside to rigorous analysis. It is hoped that this book will go some way toward filling the gap. The account which follows does not purport to cover all aspects of, and factors affecting, rural settlement and land-use patterns of location: it is an essay in the logical development of a closely related set of ideas. From the analysis it is evident that certain themes recur at all scales of consideration and under very diverse conditions of the physical environment and of economic development. An attempt is made to examine some of the practical conclusions which emerge from the argument.

I wish to acknowledge the debt I owe to those at Cambridge who taught me, in particular Mr A. A. L. Caesar. I also owe much to my former colleagues at the Institute for Research in Agricultural Economics, Oxford, and especially the Director, Mr C. G. Clark, for much help and stimulation. To Professor W. G. East, Editor of this series, I am grateful for many helpful comments and suggestions; to Mr K. A. Sinnhuber, PH.D., particularly for help with Chapter 2; Professor M. J. Webb and Mr G. Manners for discussion, comment and criticism; finally Mr R. A. Phillips for assistance with the illustrations. But mine alone is the responsibility for any sins of omission or of commission.

M.C.

I

INTRODUCTION

Of recent years there has been a growing awareness of, and interest in, the problems presented by distances between places on the surface of the earth. Much of this interest has been stimulated by the issues involved in planning a reasonable distribution of employment opportunities in the different parts of this and other countries; more recently, there has been a spectacular expansion of interest in economic growth and the problem of getting the 'under-developed' countries to the point of 'take-off' into sustained growth. Such matters involve the relative advantages of locations, both in connection with their natural resources and their position relative to other parts of the world. Sociologists and town planners and others have become acutely aware of the social difficulties which arise from a long daily journey to work due to the separation of dwellings and workplaces. One of the objectives in planning is to reduce the amount of circulation necessary for the conduct of the normal business of living. Geographers have for long claimed an interest in the differences which exist between places and there is an increasing awareness among them that many observable variations of phenomena in space are attributable to relative locations rather than to the intrinsic qualities of the individual places. In many other fields of study and endeavour, such as economics and the organization of retail trade, the problems associated with distance and circulation are receiving increased attention; witness of this is given by studies of the influence of distance upon international trading patterns and the care taken in locating the large peri-urban shopping centres which are being built in the United States and elsewhere.

Distance, then, is the central theme around which this book is written, in an attempt to provide a systematic account of certain features of rural settlement and land use. By developing a systematic study, it has been possible to draw upon a wide range of seemingly unrelated materials to show how these have certain elements in common. In doing this, no claim is made to have elaborated a general theory of universal validity, because the problem of distance is only one among many factors affecting location patterns. However, it is a factor which has its influence everywhere in the world in all location matters, even if at times it is of negligible importance. To obtain a complete understanding of a location problem, the nature of the effects of distance must be appreciated. Though in some cases it may not be very important, it usually has a considerable influence and is often the dominating consideration.

The genesis of this book throws light on another aim which I had in mind when writing. For several years I was responsible for teaching Land Economics for a Diploma in Agricultural Economics[1] and this presented an interesting problem in the choice of material and approach. Many of the persons taking the Diploma came from abroad, the majority subsequently becoming engaged in various forms of administrative or advisory or research work in connection with agriculture under very diverse conditions. It was clear that an exposition of the economics of land use had to be couched in terms of principles with a universal application, backed with suitable examples, such that the students would subsequently be able to apply the concepts to their own particular problems. It was also necessary to present the ideas in a manner which would enable their relevance to day-to-day problems to be seen readily; abstract theory would be a waste of time. I was further led to the conclusion that the central problems in the economics of land use can be stated quite simply as problems of location, of the competition between alternative users and uses to command each particular site.

This train of thought led to the issue of how best, in a limited amount of time, to introduce ideas on location to those unfamiliar with such studies. I chose to use a common situation which has an evident bearing on agricultural problems over the greater part of the globe: a particular farmer operates a holding which instead of being included within a single boundary is split up into several

[1] Superior figures refer to end-of-chapter notes.

fragments which lie at various distances from the dwelling. On the one hand, there are all the problems arising from the general loss of time, cost of fencing and inability to use machinery properly. On the other, there is the effect of distance upon the way in which each plot of land is used. It is easy to show why it is rational to arrange the type of farming on each plot so that on the furthest ones the amount of labour which has to be bestowed is the least, with a consequential ordering of the crops and methods of cultivation in relation to distance from the farmstead.

The next step was to show that exactly the same sort of thing is manifest at larger scales, influencing the regional patterns of agriculture and indeed world distributions of crops and farming systems.

Hence, my concern has been to examine what really does happen in practice and to couch the exposition in terms designed to have relevance to practical matters. Though a certain amount of theoretical analysis is necessary to provide a framework for the body of the text, theory has been accorded the minimum of attention consonant with the general aim. Thus, no comprehensive account of the literature on location is offered, though it is hoped that what is given provides a coherent and intelligible outline. Those seeking a survey of the literature and of the development of location ideas are referred to such works as Ponsard's *Histoire des Théories Économiques Spatiales* and *Économie et Espace*[2] and Isard's text *Location and Space Economy*.[3] On the other hand, there is nothing inherently complicated in the ideas expounded in this book and the techniques required to pursue their study are neither elaborate nor highly subtle. As has been already hinted, the exposition has relevance for persons engaged in a wide range of occupations; it is hoped that it will interest not only geographers and agricultural economists but also economic historians and engineers, sociologists and planners, and others besides.

It has been assumed that the reader is not a trained economist and is therefore unfamiliar with the technical terminology of this subject. Accordingly, every attempt has been made to minimize the use of technical terms, and where their use cannot be avoided, to give some definition of the expressions employed. It is hoped that these measures have been radical enough to achieve their purpose, of rendering the following pages readily intelligible to the non-economist. The reader familiar with the economist's vocabulary may feel impatient with occasionally cumbersome phrases, or ones that are not strictly precise; may he forbear, curbing his impatience in the interests of other readers, for I do not think that any great solecisms have been committed.

Types of location studies

Two major threads may be discerned regarding the methods and purposes of location studies, the one most unlike the other. Of these, the first to notice are studies in which one individual firm is the centre of study, or perhaps several such, and the object is to examine all the factors which have been important in determining the location thereof. This may be done by interviewing the managers, asking them for their opinions on what influenced the decision to locate at A rather than B or C, and by examining the cost structure to determine by how much profits at A are greater than they would be at B or C, and for what reasons. The result of such studies will be the listing of all the significant factors, with an attempt to assess the relative importance of each. This assessment must normally be a qualitative judgment, as very unlike factors are being compared, to which it may not be possible to put a money measure. The conclusions are specific to the particular firm and do not have any general value, unless: (1) the particular firm studied is representative of many similar ones, or (2) enough results can be collected for generalization to be possible. Such studies are invaluable as a means of testing hypotheses and building up a body of factual knowledge, but of their nature they do not provide a framework of concepts and methods of analysis applicable in a wide range of situations. Such concepts can be obtained only from *a priori* reasoning on evidence collected in this and other ways.[4]

Radically different is the school of thought elaborated by Lösch[5] and Isard,[6] in an attempt to develop a general theory embracing all the important factors and adequate to explain all the main features of spatial distributions. This approach tends to concentrate attention upon what patterns ought to be rather than what they are. Lösch in particular develops his theories regarding the nature of the ideal distributions and then seeks evidence that in fact reality does conform. To a large extent, it is the urban and industrial sectors of the economy which have been subjected to this form of scrutiny though recently agriculture has been served in the same manner by Rullière and Klatzman.[7] They work out a number of formulae whereby it is intended to be possible to predict the rational type of agriculture which ought to be pursued in all areas if the characteristics of soil,

climate, transport costs, etc., are known. This type of work seeks
to investigate the interrelationships between all the elements of the
economy in a quantitative manner; from this study, a model can
be constructed which will serve to predict what ought to happen in
any given circumstances. Either the best location for a firm can be
obtained, or the best use for a particular piece of land; all the
adjustments which are required in the rest of the economy can be
predicted and the over-all spatial patterns can be derived. General
theories of this kind, or theories of general equilibrium, suffer from
several defects, of which three may be noted:

(1) Necessarily, they are formulated in mathematical and algebraic
terms, so that they require considerable expertise in these fields.
Hence, they are accessible only to experts.

(2) More important, because affecting the fundamental basis, is
the necessity for a high level of abstraction from reality. To express
the data in mathematical terms, assumptions have to be made
which are often dubious.

(3) Closely related to (2) above, factors to which suitable quantities cannot be assigned are perforce ignored. Consequently, it is
not possible to take account of all phenomena, and 'exceptions'
must in fact occur. The result is that any theory of general equilibrium must necessarily be unreal to some extent, pertaining to an
assumed world which to a greater or lesser degree diverges from
the actual one. Such a theory is not really designed to give guidance
in particular cases, because the analytical process is so very complex; rather, it is designed to study the general pattern.

For their particular purposes, the above two approaches are useful
and necessary, but they leave between them a large middle ground
for which neither is suitable. This book is at once more ambitious
and more modest; more ambitious than cataloguing factors, more
modest than attempting a general equilibrium analysis which seeks
to explain all phenomena. It is, in fact, a reversion to the method
from which Lösch and Isard built up their systems, the method of
partial equilibrium. With this method of analysis, certain data are
assumed to be given, being fixed points of reference. Other phenomena are then allowed to vary, the consequential location patterns
being observed for each particular set of circumstances. By this form
of reasoning, only incomplete answers are vouchsafed because no
attempt is made to account for the data which are assumed to be
given. For example, we may assume that the location of London is
fixed and hence the location of a very big consuming centre. We may

then proceed to examine the influence which this city has upon the disposition of agricultural production, having regard to the cost of transport and the physical conditions of the land and climate. This would be an analysis in partial equilibrium, with physical conditions and the location of London as fixed and known quantities. An altogether more complicated problem would be involved if it were allowed that the disposition of conditions for plant growth in this country and elsewhere, influencing the cost of feeding our capital, could, even to an infinitesimal degree, alter the location of London. We would then be involved in calculations of the mutual repercussions of a series of small adjustments in location, such that any slight shift in one necessarily influences the other which in turn reacts upon the first, and so on. One must either be content with an answer derived from successive approximations, which can never be completely accurate, or devise a series of equations suitable for simultaneous solution. The more variables that are introduced, the more complex becomes the solution to such a problem.

Religious belief provides a parallel sort of issue. Believers are content to accept the existence of a god or deity as a 'fact' and to base their attitudes and actions upon this foundation. They have a point of reference in their lives about which everything else can be arranged. The sceptic may want to know how it is possible to conceive of a First Cause—how was it itself caused? He may insist that there is no such thing as a First Cause, only an endless chain of interacting causes, each having some influence on all others. A disturbance in any one cause must have its repercussions on all others, until some new equilibrium is attained, if indeed that is possible. For the believer, the First Cause is not subject to influences from elsewhere in the chain of causation. By this analogy, analysis by partial equilibrium corresponds to the situation of the believer, by general equilibrium to the position of the sceptic.

The use of the simpler approach of partial equilibrium may be justified on several grounds. There are the problems associated with more general theories which have already been mentioned. Second, it is purposed to frame this account with respect to what does actually occur, or is likely to happen in the future, and not with respect to what ought to arise in some locationally ideal world. In doing this, the concern is necessarily with the decisions which people take in the light of the knowledge which is available to them. Hence, third, it is entirely reasonable when considering agricultural matters to assume that certain things are given and immutable, at any rate in the short run. The most obvious example is that the conditions of the physical environment can only be altered to a very small extent by human agency, whether deliberate or not. Recent experiments with the 'seeding' of clouds to induce rain have had only a limited success and it seems quite apparent that no fundamental climatic change can be brought about. Geological and topographical conditions also are not subject to alteration, except marginally. Admittedly, there are slow changes taking place in the physical environment independently of human interference, such as the isostatic readjustment of the level of several land masses following the diminution of the ice caps at the end of the Ice Age. On the human time scale, such changes are usually too slow to be noticed by any one generation. For most practical purposes, it can be taken that natural conditions are unchanging: this eliminates the problem of variation in one set of factors, and so much simplifies the whole problem of location analysis.

It is also generally possible to regard the location of the major urban areas as fixed. In most cases, the situation of urban centres is based very largely on industrial and commercial opportunities, though some regard must be had for the ease or otherwise of obtaining foodstffs. Even when agricultural raw materials are included with foods, it remains true that in the majority of cases location with respect to agricultural supplies has very little influence on the location of the major urban areas, except in the broadest regional sense that fertile areas can support dense populations and vice versa. Normally, differences in locational advantages with respect to agricultural supplies are reflected in variations in the prices which have to be paid for the produce: a good location means low prices, a poor one high prices. Hence, for many purposes it is entirely reasonable to assume that the major urban areas have developed in their present situations for reasons which need not be considered, their existence being accepted as a fact.

As will become apparent in subsequent chapters, it is quite reasonable to assume the fixity of certain phenomena at all scales of consideration. It may be the farmstead which is taken as given, an urban centre or a major industrial region such as the Ruhr. The same is true of other factors, such as the quality of the soil, which varies from field to field, region to region and between different parts of the world.

The method of presentation which has been adopted is to take a situation at a moment in time, when it may be assumed that techniques are unchanging, and to analyse the location patterns which occur. In the body of the book, the idea of technical change is only conveyed incidentally, by discussing a sequence of situations succeeding each other in time (see Chapter 5 in particular). A systematic discussion of changes in techniques is reserved to the end. Notice also the segregation of material according to the scale of phenomena, large or small, rather than according to the 'subject' as conceived along orthodox lines of distinction, e.g. the study of settlement types and farm management. Classification by scale of phenomenon serves the purposes of showing how outwardly unrelated things do have close affinities in certain respects and it obviates a great deal of otherwise necessary repetition. It is also important to emphasize the relevance of what follows at all periods in time, a point which is made by using material from the historical past as well as from the present day.

The next two chapters are devoted to an account of some aspects of location theory as developed by earlier workers, providing a framework of concepts which are then applied by showing how they work in reality. It must be emphasized that this exposition is not a complete account of the literature; in fact, attention is concentrated upon two authors, von Thünen and Weber, whom one may regard as the founders of location analysis. Theirs is the method of partial equilibrium analysis that has tended to fall out of favour with the more recent attempts at general equilibrium theories. Chapter 2 is devoted exclusively to an account of the ideas of von Thünen, for two reasons. His ideas are central to the theme of this book and provide the greater part of the conceptual background. Second, even in translation, von Thünen is difficult to read and most of the summaries that have been published pick on only one part of his argument, ignoring the remainder, which both amplifies and qualifies his conception of the concentric zoning of land use around a single market centre. This account is therefore offered as a means of preparing the ground and in the hope of clearing away some misconceptions.

BIBLIOGRAPHICAL NOTES

1. At the Institute for Research in Agricultural Economics, Oxford.

2. C. Ponsard, *Histoire des Théories Économiques Spatiales*, 1958; *Économie et Espace*, 1955, translated into English and published as *History of Economic Location Theory*, 1967.

3. W. Isard, *Location and Space Economy*, 1956.

4. See, for example, M. L. Greenhut, *Plant Location in Theory and Practice*, 1956.

5. A. Lösch, *The Economics of Location*, English ed., 1954.

6. W. Isard, 1956, *supra*.

7. G. Rullière, *Localisations et Rhythmes de l'Activité Agricole*, 1956; K. Klatzman, 'La localisation rationelle des productions agricoles', *Metroeconomica*, 1958, pp. 33–45.

2

JOHANN HEINRICH VON THÜNEN

A point of fundamental importance to the understanding of what follows in this chapter is the fact that the ideas developed and expounded by von Thünen do *not* constitute a theory of location. They amount to a method of analysis which may be applied to any situation in any time or place, and von Thünen himself was at pains to make it clear that his particular findings had no claim to universality. But, he claimed, the method by which these results were obtained could be applied generally. It is the failure to grasp this basic point that has caused many writers to reject von Thünen's ideas as of historical interest only, having no application to modern situations. It is from this initial proposition, that it is the method and not the particular finding which counts, that the character of this chapter derives; an essay in *a priori* reasoning.

Von Thünen published his major work, *The Isolated State*, in 1826,[1] with the avowed aim of discovering the laws which govern the prices of agricultural products and the laws by which price variations are translated into patterns of land use. His was the approach of a practical farming man, for he owned and very successfully operated the estate of Tellow, near Rostock; a point of considerable interest to him was to discover the financially most rewarding system for conducting his enterprise.

His argument started from the premise that the areal distribution of crops and livestock and of types of farming depends upon competition between products and farming systems for the use of any particular plot of land. On any specified piece of land, the enterprise which yields the highest net return will be conducted and competing enterprises will be relegated to other plots where it is they which yield the highest return. Von Thünen was, then, concerned with two points in particular: (1) the monetary return over and above the monetary expenses incurred, by different types of agriculture;(2) such net returns pertaining to a unit area of land and not to a unit of product. For example, if a comparison is being made between potatoes and wheat, we will not be concerned with the financial return obtained per ton of product but with the return which may be expected from a hectare of land in either crop. Thus, at certain locations wheat may be less profitable than potatoes because, although the return per ton on wheat is higher than on potatoes, the latter yield perhaps three times the weight of crop to a hectare of land. In this case, potatoes will occupy the land.

Economic Rent

The actual process of competition for the use of land is more complicated than is suggested in the last paragraph and to analyse the matter von Thünen introduced the concept of Economic Rent, a concept which had been propounded by Ricardo a few years previously. At the time of preparing his first draft, von Thünen was unaware of Ricardo's work, though by the time the first edition of *The Isolated State* was completed he had read Ricardo. Though von Thünen arrived at the concept of Economic Rent independently of Ricardo, the idea, and particularly von Thünen's version of it, had been briefly stated a century and a half earlier by Sir William Petty.[2] Economic Rent, it must be stated at once, is not the same concept as the term 'rent' in ordinary usage, rent denoting the payment which a tenant makes for the right to occupy a farm or dwelling or other property. It is unfortunate that the two terms are widely used: as they both have common currency, some explanation of the concept of Economic Rent is essential to the exposition.

The Ricardian argument regarding the nature of Economic Rent may be recapitulated in the following manner. Imagine a town which has a certain demand for wheat, a requirement that can be met by cultivating only the best quality of land in the vicinity. This, we will say, yields 2 metric tons per hectare per annum. Suppose that the population of the city grows, with a consequential rise in the demand for wheat. All the best farmland is already in use and it is necessary to press into service terrain of a lower fertility, yielding only $1\frac{1}{2}$ tons per hectare. We will assume that the cultivation costs of grade A land are the same as for grade B, irrespective of the differing yields. We now have the situation in which farmers occupying grade A land get a $\frac{1}{2}$ ton of wheat more than their neighbours on each hectare they farm, and for no greater outlay. Now it would be worth the while of a farmer on grade B land to offer a farmer on grade A soil anything up to a $\frac{1}{2}$ ton of wheat a year for the right to cultivate a hectare of this better land. This $\frac{1}{2}$ ton represents the 'surplus' which the farmer operating the better land obtains through applying his labour there rather than on the poorer land. Let us now suppose that all the land belongs to one landlord. Farmer Y on the B quality land may go to him offering to pay $\frac{1}{4}$ ton a hectare for the land currently farmed by X on the better land. At the time Y goes to the landlord, nobody pays him anything for the use of the land they cultivate. If the landlord accepts the offer, Y will now obtain 2 tons from each hectare but will have the additional expense of the $\frac{1}{4}$ ton given to the landlord; this will leave him better off by as much as a $\frac{1}{4}$ ton. On the other hand, farmer X will now have to cultivate some of the poorer soil, from which he will obtain only $1\frac{1}{2}$ tons per hectare; he will be worse off by $\frac{1}{2}$ a ton. It would therefore be to the advantage of farmer X to offer the landlord somewhat more than a $\frac{1}{4}$ ton to retain the use of his A quality land. If farmer Y offered more, it would be worth the while of X to raise his own bid as high as a $\frac{1}{2}$ ton, which is the highest figure to which Y could go. At this figure, both farmers would be getting the same return and the 'surplus' which accrues to the better land would be taken by the landlord.

In the imaginary case cited above, Economic Rent is a $\frac{1}{2}$ ton a hectare on the better land and nothing on the poorer. It is equivalent to the surplus production that can be obtained from the use of the better soil above the return which could be obtained by applying the same resources of labour etc. to the poorer land. As there is plenty of grade B soil, some of which is not used, this gives no Economic Rent. However, if the urban population grows still further, it may be that all the grade B land is cultivated and that the next poorer soil, grade C, must also be utilized, the latter yielding only 1 ton of wheat per hectare. If we assume that the cultivation costs of this inferior land are the same as on the superior grades, a simple repetition of the steps of the above argument will show that the best land now has an Economic Rent of 1 ton per hectare while the middle grade now has an Economic Rent of a $\frac{1}{2}$ ton. In other words, the Economic Rent of a particular piece of land is the return that can be obtained above that which can be got from the land which is at

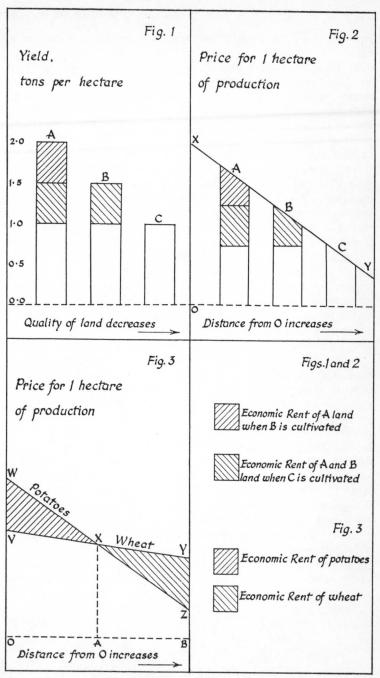

Figs. 1–3   The nature of Economic Rent

the margin of economic cultivation. The position is illustrated in Fig. 1.

In the above exposition, the idea of tenants paying landlords for the use of land has been employed, yet previously a distinction was drawn between Economic Rent and the rental payments which people actually make. This need not be confusing if it is remembered that the Ricardian exposition assumes a perfect degree of adjustment in all parts of the economy at all times. Under such circumstances, the rental payment which farmer X would make for the use of grade A land would equal the Economic Rent and this would be a $\frac{1}{2}$ ton per hectare when only the B quality soil was being used in addition and 1 ton when grade C land was also cultivated. In practice, there are innumerable imperfections in the way the economy works so that it is usually accidental if the actual rental payments equal the Economic Rent. But it is the level of Economic Rent which in the long run tends to determine what will be paid for the use of any parcel of land. The kind of hindrance which occurs in practice may be illustrated by two closely related examples. Until recently, the rentals of certain classes of residential property in Great Britain were controlled at levels which in some cases were the ruling levels of pre-1914; thereby, the rentals which many persons actually paid were much depressed compared with what they would have been in the absence of the controls. By contrast, the post-1945 regulation of land use has restricted the amount of land available for residential building, whereby prices have become much inflated. A third example is that the rents of many farms in the Netherlands are controlled at levels which are nominal.

It is, therefore, the concept of Economic Rent which underlies all questions of competition for the use of land and provides the means whereby this competition is resolved to provide patterns of land use. But the above account sketches only the outlines of the concept. Those who wish to pursue the matter further are referred to any of the standard textbooks on economics. It will be sufficient to notice here that the above argument has been based on the notion of the surplus that can be obtained by the employment of labour (or other inputs) on one particular piece of land instead of on a plot at the *extensive* margin of cultivation. Economic Rent also arises with respect to the *intensive* margin of land use, and also with respect to additional doses of labour (or other inputs, such as fertilizers) on the same piece of land. There is not the space here to explore these avenues, nor is it necessary to do so for the purpose in hand.

Von Thünen observed that Ricardo based his argument about the nature of Economic Rent on differences in the inherent fertility of the soil, but that exactly the same phenomenon arises if the 'quality' of the soil varies not with respect to fertility but with respect to location. The point will be seen quite readily by comparing Fig. 1 with Fig. 2. In the latter, three locations, A, B and C, are shown, situated at increasing distances from the consuming city at O. The vertical axis shows the price that can be obtained for the produce of one hectare of land under wheat. At O, this price is OX, but as the distance from O increases the price declines on account of the cost of transport to the market, this declining price being shown by the sloping line XY. (It is assumed that the yield per hectare is constant at all locations.) The shaded portions of the columns represent the level of Economic Rent at A and B if the next poorer location is cultivated. These shaded sections represent the limiting amount it would be worth the while of a farmer to pay as a rental to retain the use of the land he farms, under conditions of perfect adjustment throughout the economy.

It is but a short step to Fig. 3, in which the Economic Rent of wheat and potatoes at various locations is compared. The shaded portion VWX represents the Economic Rent yielded by potatoes with respect to wheat and the portion XYZ the amount of Economic Rent of wheat in relation to potatoes. Under these circumstances, potatoes will be grown between OA and wheat between AB. If we imagine the same sequence of crops being found in all directions about the central city, we have an inner belt of potato cultivation and an outer one of wheat production.

A fundamental element of this analysis is the facility with which a commodity can be transported. Potatoes yield a large bulk per hectare, much greater than does wheat. If a hectare of land is at a certain distance from the market, the cost of transport per *hectare* would be considerably greater for potatoes than for wheat. It is, therefore, advantageous if potatoes are grown nearer the market than wheat. This is doubly so when it is remembered that potatoes command a lower price per unit weight than does wheat. The other important aspect of this matter is the perishability or otherwise of the produce. Where deterioration is rapid, there is a great gain from being near the market because spoliation is reduced or eliminated. Consequently, perishable goods yield an Economic Rent which declines very sharply as the distance from the market increases, much more sharply than for other products; therefore, they tend to be located near the consuming centre.

So far, we have considered only the substitution of products as distance from the market increases. An alternative adjustment is to grow the same crop in a different manner, which will have the effect of altering production costs. Under any particular system of farming, it is possible to vary the level of inputs—such as fertilizers—to a considerable extent. By the 'law' of diminishing returns, each successive increase of inputs yields a smaller increment of production than the last. Under these conditions, if we move towards the market from a distant place, it becomes worth while to intensify production, in so far that savings in transport costs compensate for higher production costs. There will come a point when the advantages to be had from intensifying further the particular system of farming are more than offset by the gain which could be had from an altogether different system. This may be illustrated quite simply. Arable farming with a rotation of cash crops and no livestock is normally an unintensive system of farming compared with an economy based on a rotation of cash crops and grass, the latter being fed to livestock. Both systems can be more or less intensive, but the latter offers much greater scope for raising the output per hectare. In Fig. 3, substitute for wheat rotation arable farming without livestock and for potatoes ley farming with livestock. There is, therefore, a spatial distribution of farming systems as well as of products. Generally— but not exclusively—those systems which have large inputs oι manure, labour etc. are found near the market and the more extensive ones further away. The exceptions are of two kinds: (1) when the production from a hectare is very large despite small inputs, and of small value, as in the case of forestry at the time von Thünen wrote (see p. 28); (2) a large quantity of inputs yields a small bulk of valuable end-product, as with butter. The former may be situated near the market, the latter at a considerable remove.

The Isolated State

To develop these ideas, von Thünen conceived the idea of a state which had no trade connections with any other nation and was therefore surrounded by an uncultivated wilderness. Within the confines of this imaginary state, the soil was of uniform fertility and there was a single city located centrally, all other habitations being rural. No lines of improved communication crossed the level plain,

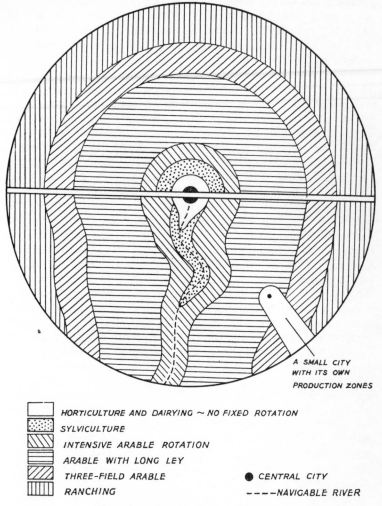

A SMALL CITY
WITH ITS OWN
PRODUCTION ZONES

HORTICULTURE AND DAIRYING ~ NO FIXED ROTATION
SYLVICULTURE
INTENSIVE ARABLE ROTATION
ARABLE WITH LONG LEY
THREE-FIELD ARABLE
RANCHING

● CENTRAL CITY
– – – – NAVIGABLE RIVER

Fig. 4   Von Thünen's system of land use

all goods transport being by horse-drawn carts. Von Thünen then
proceeded to examine data collected over a five-year period from his
own estate pertaining to the costs of production of various goods, the
yields obtained, the costs of transport to market and the ruling

market prices. On this basis, he calculated the Economic Rent accruing to each type of land use at various distances from the central city and thereby obtained an ideal distribution of production as a series of concentric circles arranged about the central city. His findings are illustrated in Fig. 4.

A point which many writers have seized upon is the fact that von Thünen put forestry as the land use occupying the zone second from the central city, whereas certain types of agriculture were put at greater distances. This arrangement accords so ill with the reality of location patterns in the developed parts of the world in the mid-twentieth century that people are often tempted to reject the whole analysis. A few explanatory words are therefore in place. At the time von Thünen wrote, forest products were in great demand for building and, more particularly, for fuel. Large quantities of timber were required for these purposes and consumers were not willing to pay high prices. A hectare of land produced a very large quantity of lumber, even though few inputs were applied; the bulky material incurred high transport costs. Thus, the advantages of proximity to the market were such that all other types of agricultural use, except the innermost zone of intensive production, were displaced by forestry; it produced a higher Economic Rent than any other product in the second zone. For the time at which he wrote, this arrangement was entirely logical. Since then, technical conditions have changed and forestry has been ousted from much of the land near the urban centres. This does not undermine the method by which von Thünen arrived at his circles.

In the first part of his work, von Thünen presented the model of his 'isolated state' for which he postulated ideal conditions. He then proceeded to use this model as a tool by which he could examine the effects of other variables, to see how they modify the 'ideal' pattern of rural land use. He was keenly aware that there is a host of other factors which all have their influence on the location of agricultural production. The 'isolated state' was never meant to be something that could really exist; indeed, he originally planned to call the work Der Ideale Staat, the Ideal or Imaginary State. Once the ideal had been established, deviations from it could be analysed.

There are first of all three points concerned directly with production costs. In his analysis, von Thünen included as a part of production costs the remuneration of the farmer, or that income of the farmer which ensures a 'normal' living wage. In imagination, we may consider this to be the wage which the farmer pays himself for his own labour, equivalent to what he would have had to pay a labourer to do this work. Von Thünen expressed wages in terms of agricultural products, so that as distance from the central city increased and prices generally tended to decline, monetary wages also fell: but the standard of living remained constant in all parts of the 'isolated state'. This opens up the possibility that the symmetry of his circles will be disturbed if in fact farmers in one part of the country have ideas regarding their just reward that differ from those who inhabit other regions. For example, farmers living near the margin of cultivation may accept a lower standard of living than those nearer the central city; this will depress the cost of production in the marginal areas and enable cultivation to be pushed further into the remoter areas than otherwise would be the case. An example of this is provided by inhabitants of the Appalachian Mountains in the United States who have a very meagre standard of living compared with that in most other parts of the country. This can only happen in an economy which is not perfectly adjusted.

The second point in connection with production costs was the observation that many inputs vary in price from one place to another, especially those which originate from the central city. The item which von Thünen particularly had in mind was manure. At that time, urban transport depended upon horses; these yielded a plentiful supply of fertilizer which was evacuated to the surrounding countryside. Because of the cost of transport, this manure became progressively more costly as distance from the city increased, until the point was reached at which it ceased to be profitable to purchase manure. This factor, combined with the bulk and perishability of the articles produced, determined the limit of the inner zone of agriculture. However, other kinds of input were included, such as the medical and legal services which all citizens require, the costs of which vary in space.

Third, the soil is not of uniform fertility, and therefore production costs vary substantially. Von Thünen showed that the variability of soil fertility has as big an effect on the location of production as the factor distance. He also noticed the importance of climate in this context, affecting as it does the costs of plant and animal production in various locations. Implicit in this point—and in the others also—is the possibility that where large differences in these factors occur they may be the dominating factor in crop distributions. However, this does not negative his analysis: it merely means that the question of distance which he analysed operates in conjunction with other factors; a *complete* explanation of a particular situation must include this factor of distance, even though in particular cases it be largely obscured by other considerations.

In his initial formulation, von Thünen assumed that the cost of transport was proportional to distance. He later relaxed this assumption somewhat, examining the situation which arises when an improved means of transport is introduced, such as a navigable river or canal, by which transport costs are less than by overland cart. Although the cost of transport along such a route was assumed to be proportional to distance, a journey which used two or more means of transport could involve different costs for the same distance; the actual cost would depend on the proportionate distance travelled by each medium. This line of better communication was assumed to run through the city (see Fig. 4). The zones of production expanded along the line of the river, while contracting elsewhere. He also considered the effects of such things as mountain barriers and import duties upon the costs of moving goods. Thus distance must be thought of as economic distance, not merely physical distance; it is the cost incurred and not the distance in so many kilometres which matters.

Von Thünen also abandoned the assumption that there is a single city. He introduced into his analysis a subsidiary city and discussed the manner in which the zones of production are modified. Though he did not press the matter, the idea of a secondary city opens up the possibility of numerous towns of roughly equal importance with production zones which mingle and mutually modify each other. The result, which is common in the real world, is a pattern of extreme complexity, but the difficulty in unravelling the details does not destroy the underlying principle. In Chapter 5 it will be shown that while for practical purposes zoning around individual cities may be rudimentary or indistinguishable, it is relevant to consider aggregations of such cities as single units about which zones of production occur.

Finally, a number of other factors was explored by von Thünen as modifications to his general scheme, notably the rôle of trade restrictions, subsidies and taxes. All of these, to a greater or lesser extent, impinge upon the prices of products and hence upon locations of production.

Subsequent workers have taken up the ideas of von Thünen and have sought to introduce improvements. These have not affected the fundamental principles but have attempted to add precision to their formulation and to bring some of the assumptions more nearly into line with reality. We need not concern ourselves with these refinements, for, while important in some respects, they do not add to an understanding of the underlying idea and are not necessary for the arguments of the succeeding chapters. The reader who wishes to pursue the matter further is referred to *The Economics of Location* by A. Lösch and *The Location of Agricultural Production* by E. S. Dunn.

There is one aspect of von Thünen's work which has received but scant attention. The above account has been couched in terms of the best manner in which to conduct the farm as a whole, given its location, and the pattern of agricultural zones which arises as a consequence. He explicitly observed that exactly the same argument applies to the distribution of cropping, etc., *within* the farm or estate, and devoted much space to an examination of the problem at this scale. The farmer knows the price of any particular product at his farm gate (the market price less the cost of transporting the commodity to market). This, then, is the local price at the farm buildings, which form the centre of operations for the farm. The fields which lie far away from these buildings incur higher costs of operation than do the nearer plots, on account of the greater amount of time spent in travelling back and forth. If the distance is sufficiently great, there will be no profit in cultivating a particular crop on the more distant lands; at a certain distance from the farmstead, the cultivation of that crop will cease. Alternatively, the returns to be had from some other crop will, at a particular distance from the farmstead, become greater: it might be that potatoes are grown on the hither fields and wheat on the further ones. Furthermore, the intensity with which each crop is grown will decline as the distance from the farmstead increases: the farming system will vary from one part of the farm to another. There will thus be a zoning of land use within the farm which repeats certain aspects of the zoning found at larger scales.

Four consequences were noted by von Thünen. First, anyone conducting a farm or estate should look to the costs of cultivating each field and the returns obtained from it and try to arrange the pattern of cropping so that the net return obtained from each field is maximized. Second—a closely related point—for any particular type of farming system there is an optimum areal extent of holding: farm size is therefore closely related to location, this being one of the determinants of farming systems. Third, the distance from the central city at which a particular crop ceases to be grown is affected by the distance within the farm from the farmstead at which it is cultivated. For example, near the central city, wheat may be grown on the furthest fields of the farms. At greater distances from the city, the Economic Rent yielded by wheat will be less, but farmers may choose to compensate for this by reducing their production costs. This they could do by growing the wheat nearer the farmstead on fields which, because they are closer, require lower costs of cultivation. In this way, the belt of wheat production could be extended somewhat beyond the limits it would otherwise have. Fourth, there is a consequence important to the question of reorganizing farm holdings. Over much of the world, farms are fragmented, with numerous parcels lying at different distances from the farmsteads. A particular parcel may be far removed from the farmstead from which it is operated, yielding a low or even negative Economic Rent. If this parcel lies near to some other farmstead, it possesses a higher potential Economic Rent for this second farmer. If some exchange can be effected which reduces the average distance of the parcels from their respective farmsteads, then the economy of the two farms will be improved and the country as a whole will be slightly better off. This is an important benefit of farm consolidation schemes which springs straight from location principles.

The next chapter develops some further ideas relating to location and shows how the ideas contained in the preceding paragraphs may be expanded in several directions. In Chapter 4 and the following chapters particular points which have been but briefly made in the present chapter are expanded and applied to particular cases.

BIBLIOGRAPHICAL NOTES

1. J. H. von Thünen, *Der isolierte Staat in Beziehung auf Landwirtschaft und Nationalökonomie*, Rostock, 1826. There have been subsequent editions, including an expurgated version edited by W. Braeuer, 1951. An English translation appeared in 1966 as *von Thünen's Isolated State*, edited by P. Hall.

For brief (and not always complete) accounts, see: *Encyclopaedia of Social Sciences*; C. Ponsard, 1955 and 1958, *supra* (ch. 1); R. Krymowski, 'Graphical presentation of Thuenen's theory of intensity,' *Journal of Farm Economics*, 1928, pp. 461–82; O. Jonasson, 'Agricultural regions of Europe', *Economic Geography*, 1925, pp. 284–6; R. L. Cohen, *The Economics of Agriculture*, reprinted 1957; A. Grotewold, 'Von Thünen in retrospect,' *Economic Geography*, 1959, pp. 346–55; R. Sinclair, 'Von Thünen and urban sprawl,' *Annals*, Association of American Geographers, 1967, pp. 72–87.

For important elaborations, see: E. T. Benedict (Ed.), *Theodor Brinkmann's Economics of the Farm Business*, 1935; E. S. Dunn, Jr., *The Location of Agricultural Production*, 1954; W. Alonso, *Location and Land Use: Toward a General Theory of Land Rent*, 1964.

2. E. Roll, *A History of Economic Thought*, 1938, pp. 106–9.

3

MORE PRINCIPLES OF LOCATION

In his exposition of the 'isolated state', von Thünen employed one assumption of which considerable use can be made. The level of prices in the city was assumed to be known and these prices then formed the datum from which prices in all other parts of the territory were derived. In the 'isolated state', each farmer could know the price he would get for any particular commodity and the cost he would incur in taking it to the market. In effect, he could derive the farmgate price for all goods and this price formed his own local datum. Each farmer would then select that product or combination of products which yielded the greatest Economic Rent at his particular location and likewise the most suitable methods of cultivation. But there would be the further problem of allocating each field to its best use, having regard to its location with respect to the farmstead. In fact, within each farm there would be a repetition of some elements of the zoning found in the 'isolated state', centred on the farmstead.

In the 'isolated state', the farmer took his own produce to market, but the above idea is just as valid if we imagine that the farmer sells his produce to a dealer who then acts as a wholesaler in disposing of it; likewise, that the inputs which an operator buys have passed through the hands of a wholesaler and retailer. However long the chain of dealers, the price at any particular point may be regarded as fixed and beyond local control.

An example will make this point clearer. In the absence of trade restrictions, the price of wheat in international trade is effectively set by the price ruling in western Europe, which takes over half the

B

world's imports. At Buenos Aires or Sydney, the price is determined by the European price less the transport costs of shipping the grain. These ports are supplied from elevators in the interior, which in turn are supplied by the local farms, and in each case the price is related to that which can be obtained at the next higher stage of marketing, less the handling costs and dealers' profit margins.

The consequences of this situation may be seen in maps showing variations in the prices received for farm products. Such maps have been compiled for the United States, based on average prices for a number of years, and show very marked regional differences stemming from several causes, among which transport costs are important. For the period 1932–41, the price received by farmers for wheat was over 100 cents a bushel in some eastern areas, falling to below 60 cents in some parts of the mountainous western States.[1] Other examples may be found in the *Economics of Location* by Lösch.[2]

In many cases, the above principle is modified by pricing policies which have the effect of averaging prices regionally and destroying the relative advantages conferred by certain locations within the area affected by such a policy. In the United Kingdom, the prices charged for gas and electricity vary between one Board and another, but within each area do not differentiate between locations the costs of supplying which vary. The regional variations in prices British farmers receive for liquid milk do not fully reflect differences in the costs of disposing it and the actual farmgate price is nearly uniform over the country.

Such pricing policies do not prevail for all goods; even where they do, there remain certain points in the chain of marketing around which zoning may take place. In the case of milk in Britain, for example, there is no price zoning for the producer until the scale of consideration has been reduced to the individual holding, when it will be in the interest of the farmer not to conduct his dairy enterprise so far from the farmstead that the cost of production swallows up the price he receives.

A single transport artery

Another important aspect of the 'isolated state', of which again much use can be made, was the introduction of a line of communication superior to the means of transport prevailing generally. In the original case, this was supposed to be a navigable river but in later writings von Thünen recognized that it could equally well be a road or railway. (Indeed, he considered the situations in which road or rail were the general means of transport.) As he recognized, the reduction of costs of transport along such an axis would cause the zone of production nearest the city to expand in that direction, distorting the concentric circles. In practice, the adjustment is not quite so simple, for such an improvement in communications would cause a larger supply of produce to be available at the same cost for the last, or marginal, consignment, and this would tend to depress prices. This in turn would cause some contraction in the zones where the improved communications had no direct influence.

But if the new route extends far enough, the distortion of the concentric zones of production would be such that along the railway, or road or river, almost parallel belts of land use would appear. This idea has been developed by a French engineer who was apparently unfamiliar with von Thünen, in an attempt to estimate the cost of providing a communications network in part of West Africa and the economic returns to be expected from it. Bourrières[3] developed his analysis from the conditions prevailing in the Ivory Coast in the late 1930's and early 1940's. The whole economy was then based upon the export of a limited range of primary products such as cotton, palm oil and timber, which were evacuated by a single railway running inland from Abidjan, supplemented by a rudimentary network of roads. Foodstuffs were grown for local consumption but other material needs were supplied by imports. Such an economy may be found in many parts of the world, especially in areas of recent European penetration and/or settlement; Australia and Brazil provide plenty of examples of railways running inland from the coast to tap agricultural or mineral resources for export.

For practical purposes, Bourrières was able to assume that prices at Abidjan were fixed, determined by the state of the world market and not to be influenced by the Ivory Coast. He possessed data on transport costs and costs of production for the various crops, which enabled him to estimate the expected extent and disposition of production zones in relation to proposals for improving communications. These production data then provided the information necessary to determine the expected level of government revenues, which could be set against the cost incurred in providing better transport facilities. By these means, he arrived at proposals for improvements and was able to show that they would be advantageous, especially in the forested southern area, which was then already the most developed.

Scale of consideration

For the purposes of exposition, von Thünen assumed that there was a single city devoid of contact with any other urban centre. But he went on to recognize that in reality there are many centres of consumption (and sources of inputs) with competing spheres of influence, so that the regularity of the zones of production is disturbed. Many subsequent writers have seized upon this to argue that the disturbance becomes so great as to vitiate the principle. The case is that the urban centres are so numerous and so close that the interlocking of production zones becomes so complicated that in practice they cannot be differentiated, and that in any case because transport differences become negligible other factors assume predominant importance.

There are two mistakes in these arguments:

(1) Because a principle appears not to apply in one place is no reason to assume it has no relevance in all other places.

(2) Because a principle appears not to apply at one scale is no reason to assume it has no relevance at all other scales.

Although it is true that in much of Europe and the United States the urban centres are very close together and often run into each other, in other parts of the world this is far from true. Darwin and Melbourne in Australia, Medan and Palembang in Sumatra and Montevideo in Uruguay are sufficiently remote from other major towns to have the essential characteristics of the 'isolated state.' And Brazil is busy creating a brand-new capital in the middle of the Amazonian wilderness: there could be few better examples of isolation from other settlements. Or there is the point already mentioned in this chapter of the single line of communications penetrating an under-developed territory, a widespread phenomenon.

Even a cursory examination will show that it would be vain to seek zones of production around the individual cities of Great Britain: although it is evident that nurserymen are almost always located on the edges of cities, in easy reach of their customers, the production of fruits and vegetables is, apparently perversely, situated in contrasting areas such as Worcestershire and Kent. But if we take a larger scale for consideration, London, Birmingham and Manchester cease to be individual urban centres and become merely parts of a regional market. It then becomes fitting to enquire how agricultural land uses may be disposed about this large market, taking into account not only the British Isles but also all those countries with which we trade. This theme is developed in Chapter

5, where it is shown that zoning of production does occur at this scale.

At the small scale, any individual farm situated in the predominantly urban area has its own problems of spatial organization within its confines; it will remain advantageous to zone production within the holding, irrespective of the external relationships. To this we shall refer in Chapter 4.

The point which has been made in the two preceding paragraphs may be generalized as follows. Though one chooses to regard the market or source of inputs as an infinitely small point, in fact all such 'points' are areas of greater or lesser extent. To regard such an area as a point is only justified if it is small in relation to the total extent under consideration. For a centre of a given size, the area chosen for study must be appropriate; for a given area of enquiry, the size of centre chosen must be suitable.

Location of agriculture and industry

The development of location studies has witnessed a traditional division between the study of agriculture based on some of the ideas of von Thünen and the study of industrial locations based on the approach of Weber.[4] It is only recently that a serious attempt has been made to integrate the two approaches, notably by Isard.[5] He points out that the focus of interest for von Thünen and his followers has been the general pattern of land use, the aggregate of individual decisions. The Weberian approach, on the other hand, is primarily concerned with the problem of the location of an individual factory. However, there is ground common to both approaches, for Weber, Hoover,[6] Lösch[7] and others proceed to a discussion of the tendency to industrial agglomeration, which stems from the aggregation of individual choices and gives rise to industrial belts or zones. At this large scale, the von Thünen and Weberian approaches coincide in the nature of their interests; but there is also much common ground at the smaller scale of the location of the individual firm, which may be a factory or a farm.

Although von Thünen was primarily interested in identifying zones of production, his technique was based on the analysis of individual holdings and his zones represent the sum of the individual choices made regarding types of production. In the initial von Thünen model, the problem is to determine the optimum *production* for a farm the location of which is given. In the Weberian case the problem is reversed; given the type of production, what is the optimum

location? There is no difference in principle between these two
approaches: it is merely that a different factor is allowed to vary.
But the similarity goes further, in two respects. In the first place it
is not necessarily the case that the location of a farm enterprise is
given. In some cases the nature of the enterprise is determined, and
the question is where to locate? Suppose that a would-be nursery-
man had a passion for asparagus and was seeking a few hectares on
which to set up in business. Asparagus is a relatively intensive form
of agricultural production and is therefore able to pay a higher
price for land than most other kinds of agricultural enterprise. The
intending grower of asparagus would therefore be able to exercise
a wide choice in selecting his holding. Some indication of how wide
the field of choice could be is given by the fact that in the United
Kingdom there are some 7·3 million hectares of arable land, of
which only a little over 600 hectares are planted to asparagus. The
intending asparagus grower would therefore have to assess the
balance of costs and benefits in an attempt to select that location
which would maximize his income. In such a case, there is nothing
different in principle from the problem of locating a steel plant: costs
of production, costs of assembly of materials and costs of distribution to markets all need to be considered in both cases. It is only
in degree that the problems differ—in scale and the relative importance attaching to the various factors. There is a complete gradation
from the above case, in which the type of agricultural production is
given and where the problem is one of selecting the best location, to
the situation in which the location is given and the problem is to
select the best pattern of land use. In point of fact, von Thünen
recognized that one consequence of his analysis was that it provided
a tool which made it possible to determine the optimum location for
any given type of production, if all the relevant information were
available. Furthermore, manufactured agricultural products such as
butter, cheese and liquor were included in his analysis.

The second similarity between the von Thünen and Weberian
approaches lies in the following proposition. In both models it is
assumed that the following are known: location of the destination
of the produce; location of the sources of inputs (coal or manure,
etc.); and the scale of the enterprise being undertaken.[8] In addition,
in the von Thünen case the location of production is known, and
the question is to determine the best form of activity; in the Weberian case, the problem is reversed. It would be equally valid to suppose
that all the quantities were known except the first, the optimum

location of consumption given the location of production. This is a real and pressing problem for any industrialist thinking of expanding his output and wondering where to concentrate his sales effort—towards expanding consumption in the areas already served, or towards capturing new markets. It is also highly relevant to the location of agricultural settlements.

In this particular case the farmstead or village is the point to which the produce is consigned and is also the point from which inputs such as labour and manure emanate. Imagine sedentary agriculturalists colonizing a previously uncultivated land, as the European settlers in north America. They have certain basic needs which must be satisfied from the resources which they can command locally—grain, vegetables, meat, timber, etc. The land in which they are settling is varied and therefore within each farm holding there will be some land more suited to one crop and some to another. Once the holding has been laid out, it will be a genuine problem for each colonist to decide where to build his farmstead, to minimize the cost of cultivating his land and reaping the harvest. His choice will be intimately bound up with the possibilities each parcel of land offers for various kinds of cultivation, and it is the settlement which is the variable for which the optimum location must be found.

Precisely the same consideration prevails in the location of hamlets and villages and the laying out of reclamation projects. Likewise, the alignment of lines of communication with respect to the agricultural potential of the land traversed is but another application of the same principle. These and other related points are discussed more fully in Chapters 6, 7 and 8.

Imperfect adjustment

There is one point which, so far as the present author is aware, has received scant attention in the literature on location, and though not of fundamental importance is significant enough to engage our attention. It is usually assumed that each producer is fully rational and that rational behaviour consists in trying to maximize income. In which case, each farmer will choose the optimum pattern of production for any given location, or the optimum location for any given agricultural system. While accepting that there is an underlying truth in this proposition, there are certain respects germane to the present theme in which it must be modified.

Toothpaste forms a very small part of the weekly outlay of any individual and a rise in price of as much as 10 per cent will probably

have no noticeable effect upon the amount used. A similar rise in
the price of potatoes could be expected to have a decided impact on
the pattern of consumption, because potatoes are a more considerable item of expenditure and because there are substitute foods
available—the substitutes for toothpaste are mostly rather un-
pleasant! For there to be a marked decline in the consumption of
toothpaste, the price rise would have to be very great.

This simple example illustrates the general case that human response to economic circumstances does not necessarily form a continuous curve but may be discontinuous or stepped. Within limits,
the diminution in standard of living resulting from a rise in certain
prices may be too small to be noticed: within wider limits, the
trouble of adjusting one's behaviour to maximize satisfaction may
be too great to warrant the effort even though one recognizes that
resources could be better allocated. To be more specific, imagine a
series of locations which are identical in every particular except
nearness to the market and that at each location is an identical
holding operated by an equally able farmer. Under such circumstances, we should expect to find the system of farming changing as
we travel from location A, near the market, to location Z which is
the furthest away. However, it is more likely that on holdings A to
F the system of farming, and its intensity, remains the same and the
only discernible difference is that F's profits are lower than A's; but
not sufficiently for F to be aware of the fact. On the other hand,
farmer G, with an even lower income, realizes the fact, but it is not
worth his while to reorganize his holding to achieve the maximum
income possible at that location. By the time we reach farmer J,
however, the disadvantages to him of using the farming system
practised by farmers A to G have become so manifest that J has
adopted a different system which yields the maximum return possible
and there will here be a distinct change of land use. The same process
will be repeated as we proceed further from the market.

We must not, then, be surprised to discover that the response to
the problem of location may take two forms. Within certain limits
there may be nothing visible on the ground, only variations in the
profits shown on the balance-sheet. Only when these variations
exceed certain limits may patterns of land use respond. Although the
evidence is very meagre, in the following chapters every effort is
made to differentiate these two responses and to discover the critical
points at which changes in location patterns are manifest.

In practice, the problem is complicated by certain other considerations of which it is extremely difficult if not impossible to take account. These are here mentioned by way of qualification. If we allow that all farmers seek to maximize their income we are faced with the question: over what period of time? In the more arid mid-west of the United States, for example, the maximum short-term income may be obtained by the monoculture of wheat, at the expense of a deterioration of the soil which ultimately will put an end to all cropping. For a long-period maximum income from the same land a mixed system of grazing and infrequent ploughing may be necessary. Consequently, the pursuit of maximum income may lead to radically different systems on two adjacent farms, the contrast arising from the different time periods envisaged by the two farmers. In the 'isolated state,' von Thünen assumed that the fertility of the soil would at least be maintained, if not improved.

But income maximization is a doubtful concept, applicable only to the unusually energetic and ambitious operators. For the majority, it seems much more realistic to suppose that the main interest is in survival and the maintenance of an accustomed standard of living. This point has been admirably demonstrated for a group of farmers in Sweden, the majority of whom were found to be operating their holdings in a manner that was sub-optimal in some degree.[9] For this reason, it often happens that systems of land use persist in locations which would be more profitably devoted to other uses and hence the boundaries separating the various zones are imprecise. Such blurring is additional to that justified by differences in physical environment, or arising from local social phenomena such as patterns of land holding and systems of tenure.

The last few paragraphs are intended to warn the reader against seeing in the material which follows a degree of accuracy greater than in fact exists and to obviate the need for repeated qualifications throughout the following chapters. However, it will become abundantly clear that despite these qualifications there are striking regularities in location patterns throughout the world, conforming to the theoretical concepts which have been expounded.

BIBLIOGRAPHICAL NOTES

1. United States Department of Agriculture, *Regional Variations in Prices Received by Farmers*, 1953. Some of the maps are reproduced in *Farm Appraisal* by W. G. Murray, 2nd ed., 1950.

2. A. Lösch, 1954, *supra* (ch. 1).

3. P. Bourrières, 'Essai d'étude économique generale des voies de communications en pays neuf', *Annales des Ponts et Chaussées*, 1950, in various parts.

4. A. Weber, *Theory of the Location of Industries*, English translation by C. J. Friedrich, 2nd imp., 1957.

5. W. Isard, 1956, *supra* (ch. 1).

6. E. M. Hoover, *The Location of Economic Activity*, 1948.

7. A. Lösch, 1954, *supra*.

8. The question of scale of enterprise has been introduced into the Weberian model by writers such as Hoover, Lösch and Isard. The choice of location is influenced by the expected scale of output, which affects in different degree the costs of assembly of materials, production and distribution of finished products and the price received. Von Thünen ignored this matter, and it does not appear to have been considered by later writers concerned with agricultural location, largely because it is relatively un-important. The matter is discussed in Chapter 8.

9. J. Wolpert, 'The decision process in spatial context', *Annals*, Association of American Geographers, 1964, pp. 537–58.

4

THE FARM AND THE VILLAGE

In this chapter, attention will be devoted exclusively to the farm, hamlet and village. The reason for treating them together is that in many cases the pattern of land use around a hamlet or village is nothing but the sum of the patterns subsisting on individual holdings which are fragmented and scattered all over the territory of the hamlet or village. For this reason, the exposition relating to one is inextricably entwined with that concerning the others. Furthermore, the scale is of the same order of magnitude in the three cases, which is to say that the actual distances involved are roughly comparable, normally not more than a few kilometres. Arising out of this similarity of scales, the terms of the argument are identical, or virtually so, in all three cases. Therefore, separate accounts would be unnecessarily tedious.

For the purpose of this chapter, we will regard the position of the farmstead as given and known: likewise, the position of the hamlet or village, since this comprises a large number of farmsteads. We may then envisage the farm in the following terms:

(1) The farmstead, or the group of farmhouse and farm buildings, is the point of origin for all the inputs which have to be applied to the land of the farm. There the farmer and his family live, leaving the farmstead each morning for the fields and returning to it in the evening and possibly at intervals during the day. Likewise, the manure accumulates in the yard or stables and the artificial fertilizers are stored in the barn, and these and everything else which is applied to the land must be taken thence to the fields.

(2) The farmstead is also the point to which all the produce of the

farm is brought, either for consumption there or onward shipment to the local dealer or market. The farmstead may quite justly be regarded as the first point in the chain of marketing, in the sense of being a collecting and clearing centre, though actual transactions do not normally take place there.

Exactly the same model may be envisaged for the hamlet or village where the dwellings of those who cultivate the surrounding land are collected: all inputs emanate thence, all produce is consigned thither.

This is an over-simplified account which omits to consider some exceptions. For example, some produce may be shipped straight from the fields to a local factory or dealer and so never pass through the farmstead or village. Or some workers may live away from the farmer's dwelling, even in another village, and be able to proceed direct to the scene of operations for the day without recourse to the farmstead for instructions. However, these are minor modifications which do not in any essential manner impair the utility of considering the farmstead or hamlet or village as the 'isolated state' that von Thünen conceived, stripped of the complications that in reality arise from competing or overlapping market areas.

In considering the manner in which a farm is operated, it will immediately be apparent that distance is important in relation to the movement both of goods and persons, and furthermore that the former requires the latter. Discounting recent experimental work on remote-controlled tractors, the shifting of any commodity or implement implies also the translocation of at least one person. Similarly, a change in job will usually involve a change in situation. Hence, all movement on a farm may be expressed in terms of man-hours, supplemented by tractor and draught animal-hours. We can choose to think in these primary terms—that distance equals human time— or we may go one stage further and convert the cost in time into money costs. This is usually done by assigning the going hourly rate of pay to each hour used for travelling; the great advantage of doing this is that such monetary costs can be compared directly with other money costs and the money returns. The disadvantage is that in many parts of the world the market economy is not sufficiently well developed for one to be able to obtain reliable money equivalents of labour time, or other inputs, or the produce. Furthermore, the true value of the time spent unproductively travelling may be the social intercourse which is forgone and not the possibility of more production. Time spent in travelling could be put to other uses, whether these be productive or merely social, and it is these other

uses which may provide the measure of the costs involved in overcoming distance.

If a farmer behaves in a rational fashion, he will be interested in
conducting his holding so that the cost of the last unit of labour
bestowed equals the value of the additional produce which will result
from it. If in fact the cost of this last (or marginal) amount of labour
exceeds the value of the marginal return, then he will tend to curtail
his operations, and vice versa. For this over-all situation to obtain,
the same must be true of each field or parcel: if it did not, then a
simple transfer of effort from one field, where the cost of the marginal
dose of labour exceeded the value of the return, to another where the
reverse situation prevailed, would enable the farmer to increase his
product without any increment in the cost of labour. Now, the total
time involved in cultivating a field for an additional hour rises the
further removed it is, since the time consumed in travelling must be
added in. It follows, therefore, that the return from this last hour of
actual work must be greater on the more distant plot than on the
nearer, to compensate for the time spent in travelling. This will result
in a lesser degree of intensity of farming at the greater remove,
through the operation of the 'law' of diminishing returns. It is an
observed fact that in agriculture each successive dose of inputs—
say hours of work—tends to yield a smaller and smaller return as
the total amount of inputs—the total number of hours worked—
rises. Hence, the farmer will desist at a point earlier on the curve of
diminishing returns the more each actual hour of work applied to
the land costs; which is to say, the further away is the field. The
point has equal force whether or not the farmer hires any labour,
the argument applying to both wage labour and family work.

It may be objected that human beings are not entirely rational.
This is true, but neither are they fools nor do they choose to do
more work than is necessary. Perhaps more cogently, it may be
asked whether the distances involved are sufficient at the scale of
the farm and village to warrant a response in the pattern of land
use. That in fact they may be will appear from the empirical material
which will be presented shortly, but lest the particular cases be
regarded as involving exceptionally great distances it will be useful
to set them against some material showing that this is not the case.

Distances involved

At the present time, perhaps the most widespread single cause of
large distances is the fragmentation of holdings and this pheno-

menon has received a good deal of attention. It is easy to cite
extreme cases, where plots may be 10 or even 20 kilometres distant
from the farmstead; there is much less information available on the
normal or common magnitudes involved. In Europe there is very
little direct information readily to be had. On the one hand, isolated
surveys and opinions can be collected, such as the estimate that in
Finland the average distance of the fields from the dwelling is
between 1·0 and 1·1 kilometre:[1] in the Netherlands, the average
distance is 1·1 kilometre, varying from 0·8 in Utrecht to 1·4 in
Noord-Brabant.[2] On the other hand, indirect means may be used to
calculate the average distance, an exercise which has been performed
by Dovring[3] for selected countries, on the basis of median village
sizes and the average number of plots per person. Varying within
the countries from region to region, he found the theoretical average
distances to plots to be (in kilometres):

Belgium	0·3–1·0
Netherlands	0·3–1·0
Switzerland	0·3–1·0
France	0·3–2·0
W. Germany	0·3–2·0
Bulgaria	2·0
Rumania	0·7–2·5
Spain	0·3–6·0

Outside Europe, in which continent one-third or even one-half the
agricultural land is fragmented and in need of consolidation, the
problem is also acute in many regions. In his mammoth survey of
Chinese land use, Buck[4] found that in a sample of nearly 17,000
farms the average distance between farmstead and field was 0·6 kilometre, ranging from 0·3 in the Szechwan Rice Region to 1·0 in the
Spring Wheat Region. The average distance to the furthest parcels
was 1·1 kilometre for the country as a whole, varying from 0·5 to
1·8 as the respective extremes for the two named regions. A very
similar picture emerges in the case of Pakistan, where a survey of
forty villages in the Punjab showed that almost half of the 356
holdings were fragmented, and that on these the average distances
of the parcels from the main plots were:[5]

TABLE 1

PAKISTAN: AVERAGE DISTANCE OF PLOTS
FROM THE MAIN PLOT
(*in Kilometres*)

Distance in kms.	Number of holdings Actual	Per cent
Less than 0·8	70	40·2
1·0–1·6	63	36·2
1·8–3·2	30	17·3
Over 3·2	11	6·3
Total	174	100·0

It would be tedious to enumerate further examples of the magnitude of the distances arising from fragmentation. It should be noted that the above-quoted figures are averages and that therefore there will be many cases where the actual distances involved are considerably greater, and likewise many where they are less.

Another reason for the existence of great distances is a rather peculiar and much less widespread form of holding, in which the properties are very narrow and grossly elongated, with the farmstead situated at or near one end. Thus, in the Netherlands, holdings reach a length of 1·4 kilometres south-east of Rotterdam, 2·0 kilometres south of the Ijsselmeer and even 3·0 kilometres to the east of it.[6] In the Netherlands, this pattern of holding has arisen from a traditional system that developed in the Middle Ages and later, whereby the extent of the commune's territory was increased by individual operators reclaiming land at the periphery, contiguous to their own holding. But the same type of pattern occurs in some areas of recent settlement, notably in the eastern regions of Canada, where many farms are narrow and long, running back from the frontage on the St Lawrence river.[7] Or, again, in the frontier region of São Paulo, Brazil, holdings extend from stream to interfluve as thin strips of as much as 3·0 kilometres in length. Meynier[8] remarks this type of holding and observes that it is commonly associated with linear villages, villages which are nothing but a line of dwellings ranged along a road or other means of circulation.

Distances may be considerable where the land of a village is farmed as a unit, in common, a system widespread in the days of the open fields, but now of small importance, except in eastern Europe and the U.S.S.R. where collective and co-operative farms exist. Finally, where there are large estates worked from a single centre, such as the European-established plantations found in many tropical and sub-tropical regions, distances may again be considerable.

In the foregoing discussion, it has been assumed that distance can be measured as the crow-flight distance from the parcel to the farmstead. In practice, most plots have only one or two points of access and the route from these to the farmstead may be devious. Normally, therefore, the actual distances which have to be traversed are greater than indicated. In some cases this is offset where the fields are very large, as on Russian collective farms. For certain operations, such as ploughing, it does not matter if the arable area extends to a great distance, for the tractor is performing useful and necessary work while it proceeds to the further limits drawing the plough behind.

The point that, properly speaking, distance should be measured in terms of the time taken, was made by Müller-Wille,[9] who prepared a map for one village with lines showing the zones of equal time required in carting manure to the fields. It is relevant for what follows that, from this study, he concluded that when more than one hour was required the amount of manure used declined sharply. The difficulty is one of obtaining sufficient direct evidence upon the amount of time used and so, for want of better, recourse has been necessary to material using crow-flight distance.

In relation to the fact that the average distance to the cultivated land is commonly of the order of one kilometre or more and very frequently rises to three or four, it is pertinent to observe that the weight of goods moved in the course of one year is notable, contributing appreciably to the costs which distance imposes. On three French farms, practising a mixed system of cultivation, the figures for all goods moved in one year (including produce and fertilizer) were:[10]

Farm	Metric-tons per hectare
1. Gâtinais, 25 hectares	15·4
2. Aube, 144 hectares	16·5
3. Seine et Oise, 145 hectares	18·0

That these figures are likely to be representative of much of western Europe is indicated by the data available for the United Kingdom pertaining to the quantities of various agricultural items produced and the purchases by farmers of lime, fertilizers and feeding-stuffs. From these it can be estimated that the minimum quantity of all commodities handled per hectare per annum on an ordinary British farm is 7 metric tons and that the average weight is likely to be at least 10. On the other hand, in regions of extensive cultivation, especially the semi-arid parts of the world, the weight handled annually is considerably less.

As a result of the distances involved and the quantities of commodities to be moved, the proportion of all working time spent in movement is about one-third on British farms. In the Netherlands, over half the working hours of horses and tractors may be devoted to the movement of produce and materials and in south-east Nigeria the oil palm growers spend about one-third of the time they devote to farming to travel between their houses and their farms.[11] It is likely that the order of magnitude is similar in much of the rest of the world and it is therefore hardly surprising that farmers make some adjustments in the spatial pattern of their operations with the intention to economize effort.

Relation of production to distance

The importance of considerations such as the above has attracted the attention of research workers on the Continent, who have been concerned to discover the economic effects of fragmentation and the benefits to be derived from the consolidation of holdings. We will begin by discussing the results which throw light upon the influence distance has on the level of gross and net output, and then examine some of the spatially visible aspects of the matter.

A detailed survey was carried out by Wiiala[12] on a single parish in Finland, with the object of measuring the benefits to be obtained from the consolidation of the holdings. From the accounts kept by the farmers, he was able to measure the effect of distance upon the level of gross and net production, as measured in money terms. This he did by computing the average distance of the fields from the farmstead for each farm and the average return (gross and net) per hectare. He found that as the average distance increased, the per hectare returns declined, and he was able to obtain an algebraic relationship from which the figures in Table 2 have been computed. The net product declines much more rapidly than the gross output, a situation which arises from the fact that the level of costs actually incurred diminishes less swiftly than the level of gross product. His figures indicate that at an average distance of but one kilometre the gross return has fallen by 16 per cent and the net return by 44 per cent: at 2 kilometres the net return per hectare is very small.

Much the same result was obtained in another study of a Finnish community conducted by Virri,[13] in which he found a strikingly similar decline in gross yield but a somewhat different behaviour of the net yield, which declined even more rapidly for the first kilometre but less precipitately thereafter. In like manner, Suomela[14] discovered from an analysis of a sample of farms scattered all over Finland that the rapidity with which the net product declines diminishes as the distance increases. That both the gross and net product should decline with diminishing rapidity at the greater distances is to be expected. The land near the farmstead receives considerable inputs of manure as well as of labour for cultivation and therefore a large proportion of the gross yield is attributable to factors other than the inherent fertility of the soil. With increasing distance, the various inputs of fertilizers and labour become smaller and therefore an increasing proportion of the total yield arises from the natural capacity of the land, until the point is reached that even with a minimal amount of care some level of production would be maintained. The data collected by Wiiala probably do not show this tendency owing to the fact that the maximum average distance with which he was concerned was not very great, being about 2 kilometres.

TABLE 2

FINLAND: RELATION OF PRODUCTION PER HECTARE AND
DISTANCE TO FARM PLOTS
(0–0·1 Km. equals 100)

Distance in kms.	Wiiala		Virri		Suomela
	Gross output	Net output	Gross output	Net output	Net output
0–0·1	100	100	100	100	100
0·5	92	78	89	67	83
1·0	84	56	80	50	68
1·5	77	34	73	40	56
2·0	69	13	67	33	46
3·0	—	—	57	25	32
4·0	—	—	50	20	—
5·0	—	—	44	17	—

It may be objected that the reduced yield obtained on the more distant lands is a result of either or both of two factors which are correlated with distance. First, the more distant land may be poorer. In the case of the three sets of data quoted above, this was not a consideration which attracted the attention of the authors as being important and they attribute the whole diminution to distance. In any case, the method which, perforce, they had to adopt precludes this as a serious likelihood. The book-keeping data were available only for each farm as a whole and not for individual fields, so that Wiiala's method of measuring distance was adopted. While it may be the case that on an individual farm the poorer land is at a greater remove than the better, there is no evidence to suggest that in general farms with a greater average distance to the plots possess inferior soils.

The second possible cross-correlation is that those farms with a greater average distance to the parcels were also larger farms. This would affect the intensity of production, for in general the per hectare level of gross and net income falls as farms increase in size. There is some evidence to show that in the case of Finland the larger farms do have greater average distances to their plots than the smaller but this is compensated in part by the fact that the plots are considerably larger, which has the effect of reducing the disadvantageous effects of distance. It appears, then, in the cases so far cited, that the major part of the fall in yield associated with distance is attributable to distance alone.

Using essentially the same technique with the accounts of 227 farms scattered over central Sweden, Larsson[15] obtained very similar rates of decline for gross and net product. Examining the constitution of the farms, he concluded that the findings must be attributed primarily to the influence of distance and not to the quality of the soil or other factors. The following table is derived from his findings, which relate to the period 1939–43:

TABLE 3

SWEDEN: PERCENTAGE REDUCTION IN OUTPUT PER HECTARE FOR
EACH KILOMETRE INCREASE IN DISTANCE FROM THE FARMSTEAD

Size group of farms, hectares	Number of farms	Percentage decrease in output for 1 kilometre increase in distance	
		Gross production	Net production
10–20	95	4	74
20–40	85	9	50
Over 40	47	26	46
Average	—	13	57

Observe that the larger farms show a much more rapid decline for gross production than do the smaller holdings and that the converse situation holds for net product. The man with a small business must extract every bit of income he can from his property and therefore tends to push production to the maximum level possible on all his land. To maintain his level of gross output he must incur increasingly great costs of input as the distance increases. The man with a larger enterprise does not have to worry so much about obtaining the maximum total income and can afford to adjust his farming more carefully, reducing very sharply his inputs on the more distant fields. His gross product falls, but not as rapidly as his inputs. Larsson commented that this is apparent in terms of land use, the larger farms tending to have more grazing land of an unintensive nature than do the smaller holdings.

Some work done on fragmented farms in the Maas and Vaal areas of the Netherlands showed that the gross yield rose by roughly 10 per cent for each kilometre a plot was nearer to the farmstead.[16] Expressed the other way round, this equals a diminution of 9 per cent for each kilometre the parcel is removed from the farm dwelling, which is a markedly lesser rate of decline than has been found in Finland and Sweden, at least over the first 2 kilometres. Nevertheless, it indicates a decline in net product of at least 15 or 20 per cent per kilometre. The same phenomenon has been expressed in somewhat different terms with respect to those Dutch farms which are extremely long: 'investigations . . . have shown that the disadvantages of inferior cultivation of the rear portions of holdings could generally be observed in the case of a length [of the holding] of over 1,200 to 1,500 metres.'[17] This observation pertains to ordinary arable and livestock farming. For the effects to be visible on the ground, the diminution in gross product is almost certain to be at least 10 per cent, which again suggests that the net product falls by 15 to 20 per cent for each kilometre.

There are, finally, some figures relating to an entirely different milieu, the Punjab in Pakistan. In a survey of small holdings, in connection with the problem of fragmentation, 'it was noticed that cultivation operations were adversely affected due to the existence of tiny plots situated at considerable distances. . . . A previous investigation into this aspect estimated that the expenses of cultivation increase "by 5·3% for every 500 metres of distance for ploughing, from 20 to 25% for the transport of manure and from 15 to 32% for the transport of crops".'[18] The only major operation omitted is that of tending the growing crops. It is evident that, if the intensity of farming remains constant at all distances, the total cost of cultivating land rises by over 20 per cent for every kilometre, which would have the effect of reducing the net product per hectare in like measure.

Thus, there is a considerable body of quantitative evidence to demonstrate the rate at which the level of gross and net product does in fact decline with increasing distance, evidence which gives a firm basis to the numerous qualitative references to the matter which may be found in the literature. The material which has been quoted applies to technical conditions which for the most part require pedestrian human location and the common use of draught animals for ploughing and the transport of goods, for the level of mechanization was not high at the time the studies were made. These are conditions which still obtain in much of Europe and even more widely in large tracts of the world; therefore, the above-quoted estimates of the economic effects of distance are of the utmost relevance.

We are now almost in a position to examine some of the adjustments that farmers make to meet the exigencies of distance and to reduce the costs they incur in overcoming space. At the beginning of this chapter, the argument led to the conclusion that the actual level of labour input ought to diminish with increasing distance and the evidence which has been presented implies that this does in fact occur. There is some further Dutch material based on workstudy observations of the amount of time actually applied to the land—that is, with travelling time omitted. The following approximate figures have been obtained from two diagrams prepared by Visser,[19] showing a very marked decline in the actual labour input:

TABLE 4

NETHERLANDS: MAN-HOURS PER ANNUM PER HECTARE
ACTUALLY WORKED ON PLOTS OF OVER 15 HECTARES

Distance from farmstead in kms.	Grassland plots	Arable plots
0·5	220	400
1·0	210	360
2·0	180	300
3·0	160	240
4·0	130	190
5·0	110	150

It is the diminution of the actual labour input which underlies the phenomena to which we shall now turn.

Adjustment to distance

There are two important ways in which the adjustment to distance may take place: the same products may be enterprised less intensively, or there may be a substitution of products towards those which are less demanding of labour. Some evidence bearing directly on the former, and in part on the latter, is provided by numerous Dutch studies on the mineral status of the soil in plots removed various distances from the farmstead; these surveys have shown a universal tendency for the mineral status to decline with increasing distance from the farmstead, implying that this is due to the less frequent application of fertilizers. This circumstantial evidence is confirmed by some direct observations on a random sample of arable plots scattered throughout the Netherlands:[20]

TABLE 5

NETHERLANDS: PERCENTAGE OF ARABLE PLOTS RECEIVING
ORGANIC AND LIQUID MANURE

	Distance of plots from the farmstead in kms.			
	Under 0·15	*0·45–0·85*	*1·45–2·95*	*Over 2·95*
Organic manure	45	33	38	18
Liquid manure	7	10	5	3

An alternative adjustment is the substitution of less demanding products at greater distances, with a consequent change in the type of enterprise: this form of adjustment is much more readily visible on the ground and on maps. And it is at this point that we turn our attention away from the patterns of land use on farms to the patterns obtaining around villages, for the pattern of land use related to a nucleated settlement is composed of the patterns of the constituent farms and it is common, though not universal, for farms which are operated from such settlements to be fragmented. Thus, the individual farms have their own problems of internal organization in relation to distance and the pattern of land use round the centre arises from the sum of the individual decisions. In some of the following examples, discussion of the generalized pattern of use is in fact an account of the 'average' or 'typical' farm. Alternatively, in some societies it is customary to work the land in common, in which case the whole village territory, or all that which is not privately tilled, may be regarded for our present purposes as one big farm which also has its problems of spatial distribution. But whichever the case may be, the village or hamlet is the point from which emanate all the inputs which are applied to the land—notably labour —and the point to which all produce must be taken. Strictly speaking, of course, the settlement is not a point but an area; however, it is generally so small in relation to the area tilled that the exposition is in no way vitiated.

South Italy and the islands of Sicily and Sardinia are characterized by highly nucleated settlement, a phenomenon which has attracted the attention of many writers. It is by no means uncommon for the peasantry to inhabit villages or agro-towns which reach a size of 10,000 persons and to have to travel daily to work the fields which surround the settlement. It is not our purpose to enquire how this pattern has arisen, but to accept that, for such reasons as defence, avoidance of malaria and the system of land holding, it has come to pass; however, we are concerned to elucidate some of the consequences. These

large [Sicilian] settlements, where live practically all the peasants, are generally situated on hilltops or hill slopes, sometimes dominated by a ruined castle . . .

Around these settlements there is a zone of intensive tree and herbaceous crop cultivation, in small fruit and vegetable plots, forming a 'halo' of greater or lesser extent according to the size of the village. Beyond this zone extend the former fiefs or latifundia, generally devoted to cereals and pasture.

The zone of intensive cultivation is composed of small or minute properties which are fragmented and dispersed and mostly derive from leasehold concessions; they belong to all classes of the population—the wealthy, professional persons, wage workers, artisans and peasants.[21]

Despite the fact of being situated on hills, which means that the immediately adjacent land is generally of poor quality, the most intensive agriculture is conducted here.

The same situation has been excellently noted in Sardinia, of the southern plains and plateaux:

From whichever side one leaves a village, one is struck by the rigorous disposition of the various elements of the countryside into concentric zones. Around the village . . . there is a first zone in which the view is restricted, where the parcels are small and bounded by hedges of prickly pear, growing vegetables, olives, almonds and vines. But this pleasant labyrinth constitutes only a narrow belt, and suddenly there opens out a landscape which is flat and bare, without walls, without hedges, without trees: these are the arable lands. . . . Completely cultivated in the area nearest the village, this territory becomes poorer in the distance, the amount of fallow increases . . .[22]

The deterioration of the landscape with increasing distance is attributed to the factor of distance and not to poorer natural conditions. Notice that the proportion of fallow land rises as the village is left behind, and that therefore the intensity of grain cultivation is falling.

Thanks to the publication by the Italian Touring Club of land-use maps of Italy, a more precise measurement is now possible than the above description of the arrangement of land uses around the rural centres. Canicatti is a settlement of 30,000 inhabitants, distant 18 kilometres from the nearest settlement of comparable size, typical of the larger centres in the interior of Sicily; for this reason it has been chosen for particular study. The table opposite has been compiled from the relevant sheet of the land-use map (scale 1 : 200,000), and from information supplied by the Istituto Nazionale di Economia Agraria in Rome regarding the annual labour requirements per hectare of particular crops. The distance zones have been taken from the centre of the settlement. The average labour requirement in each distance zone has been obtained from the data for the crops and the relative importance of each in the various zones.

The location of the small amount of irrigated and citrus lands is determined by the very limited area which is suitable. Apart from these two categories, the pattern of land use conforms to the descriptions which have been quoted, with a particularly marked diminution in the importance of vines, olives and arable-with-trees as the distance from the centre increases; the relative decline of the other tree crops is less marked. In this particular case, 4 kilometres is the critical distance, beyond which open arable land (growing mostly wheat and barley) becomes predominant. Also evident is the decline in the amount of labour applied to each hectare as the distance increases, with again a sharp change at about 4 kilometres. The actual diminution of labour input is undoubtedly much greater than is indicated, for two closely related reasons. First, it has been assumed that the actual labour input remains the same for each crop irrespective of the distance from the centre, an assumption which is evidently not reliable, as we have previously seen. But the data with which to allow for this are not available. Second, the arable land tends to be left in fallow more frequently at greater distances and when so left requires very little attention. Thus the right-hand column of the table should

TABLE 6

CANICATTI, SICILY: PERCENTAGE OF LAND AREA IN VARIOUS USES AND ANNUAL LABOUR REQUIREMENTS PER HECTARE IN MAN-DAYS

Percentage of land area

Distance in kms. from Canicatti	Urban	Irrigated arable and vegetables	Citrus fruits	Vines	Arable with trees	Olive	Trees*	Arable, unirrigated	Pasture and productive waste†	Coppice wood	Average number of man-days per hectare in each distance zone
0–1	44·7	—	—	15·8	—	—	19·7	19·7	—	—	52
1–2	—	—	—	18·0	16·7	8·4	41·0	15·9	—	—	50
2–3	—	—	2·6	2·3	21·8	14·4	35·4	23·6	—	—	46
3–4	—	—	2·1	13·3	18·7	0·6	47·2	18·1	—	—	50
4–5	—	—	—	5·1	19·2	2·4	28·4	43·4	1·4	—	42
5–6	—	1·0	—	6·3	4·7	1·6	17·6	64·1	4·7	—	41
6–7	1·3	0·7	—	3·3	6·7	—	18·3	68·7	0·9	—	40
7–8	—	—	—	4·0	7·7	—	23·6	62·4	0·8	1·6	39
Total	1·0	0·3	0·4	6·1	11·1	2·2	26·3	50·8	1·4	0·4	—
Average number of man-days per hectare		300	150	90	50	45	40	35	5	5	42

* Mainly almond, hazel, carob and pistacchio.
† Sometimes sown.

be interpreted in the following manner: it indicates the minimum rate of reduction of labour inputs with increasing distance, and measures the magnitude of the labour economy which is actually achieved solely by the substitution of less demanding crops towards the periphery of the commune's territory, taking no account of variations in the intensity with which individual crops are grown.

Exactly the same type of situation has been noted in Spain. Of La Mancha, a particularly arid part of the Meseta south of Madrid, Birot and Dresch observed:

> On a terrain which is almost perfectly homogeneous . . . the pattern of settlement and land use is remarkably geometric. In the middle of the nude plain there are enormous villages, at times numbering only 4 or 5 in 600 square kilometres. Around the villages, the bare fields on the one hand and the olives and vines on the other are disposed in concentric circles. The latter crops [olives and vines], covering an important area, generally are not found nearer the village than 3 or 4 kilometres. There is a third and outer ring, the uncleared land abutting on the surrounding hills. In sum, there has been an annual clearance about the initial centre, devoted to grain or tree crops according to the needs of the population and the state of the market.[23]

That the figure of 3–4 kilometres should be mentioned as the critical distance separating the grain fields from the olives and vines, which is roughly the same figure obtained for Canicatti, is probably a coincidence. Much more interesting is the inversion of the spatial distribution, the arable land being close to the settlement. This may be attributed to two major considerations: in La Mancha there has not been the same fragmentation of the land into small holdings adjacent to the settlement as in Italy; and under the more severe climatic conditions the labour requirement per hectare for wheat and barley is higher than for vines and olives. The latter point was succinctly made in a study of one particular Spanish village:

> This peripheral distribution [of vines and olives] is due to the fact that the cultivation of cereals requires more frequent application of labour than does the cultivation of vines and olives; this makes it more convenient for the labourer to live nearer the arable land than the vine and olive plots, in order to reduce the time lost in travelling from his home in the village to the land he works.[24]

Comparison of the Italian and Spanish material illustrates an important consideration of wide application: the relative labour requirements of the same crops are very variable from place to place and hence the relative spatial arrangement of land uses. This is clear from data supplied by the Istituto Nazionale di Economia Agraria, Rome, a selection of which is presented below, showing the annual labour requirements per hectare for certain crops as a percentage of the requirement for wheat and barley, in different parts of Italy:

TABLE 7

ITALY: ANNUAL LABOUR REQUIREMENTS IN MAN-DAYS PER HECTARE
(*Wheat and Barley equals 100*)

Crop	Aosta	Pavia	Genoa	Arezzo	Latina	Bari	Syracuse
Wheat and barley	100	100	100	100	100	100	100
Irrigated vegetables	2,390	1,020	1,440	500	960	1,250	860
Tobacco	—	155	—	—	340–510	710	—
Tomatoes	—	195	450	—	240	—	240–760
Vines	700	400	360	240	320–390	320–360	290
Olives	—	—	125	160	70	180	140
Chestnuts	60	—	45	35	33	—	—

The broad pattern remains constant: irrigated vegetables always require a lot of labour and chestnuts very little; vines need more attention than olives. But the relative position of tobacco, tomatoes and vines is much more variable from place to place. That such large differences in the relative labour needs of crops occur within the confines of a single country shows conclusively the necessity for analysing local conditions carefully and the danger of applying in one place preconceptions based on experience elsewhere.

It may be objected that the cases of zoning which have been cited so far are very special and localized. In the next few paragraphs it is shown that the same type of phenomenon is observed elsewhere. South Spain and south Italy (with Sicily and Sardinia) represent in an extreme form the concentration of the rural population into large agro-towns but the same situation prevails to a lesser degree over much of Europe. This has been clearly shown by Dovring, who has mapped the areas of various median village sizes in Europe and European Russia. Outside the two Mediterranean countries already mentioned, the median size of village is over 1,000 inhabitants in extensive tracts of Yugoslavia, Bulgaria, Rumania, the Ukraine and the area immediately north of the Caucasus: the latter region can boast a median size of over 5,000, comparable with parts of Italy and Spain.

Hence, it is no surprise to discover that in parts of Bulgaria the zoning of production around the villages has been observed as occurring generally. Birot and Dresch refer to the phenomenon, stating that the farms are only loosely grouped into villages and are each adjacent to a plot of land used for growing vegetables, fruits, some vines and cotton. Then, very close to the village, some communal pasture lands and woodlots are found and beyond them the specialized crops which require larger amounts of labour—vines, roses and tobacco. Next again come fields farmed on a two-year rotation, supporting arable crops like wheat and maize. At the edge of the territory there may be some pioneer vineyards or rose gardens nibbling away at the forest.[25] This description relates to the situation which subsisted before the Communist government came to power, before the organization of the agricultural lands under the collective-farm system which is now virtually complete in Bulgaria. To the extent that this policy has had any effect on the settlement pattern, the tendency has been to encourage the maintenance of nucleation, even to exaggerate it further, as one means of controlling and influencing the rural populace.

Policy in the U.S.S.R. has tended in the same direction, though the disadvantageous economic consequences have been realized and some move made to mitigate the extreme ill-effects. Thus, the observation of de Laveleye[26] that 'more cognizance is taken of proximity than of the (natural) fertility, since in Russia this does not vary much within each region' has been endorsed by subsequent writers and is still generally true, giving rise to a concentric arrangement of land uses.

Though in Britain there are not the large agro-towns which are found elsewhere in Europe, this does not mean that the phenomena which have been discussed in the previous pages are absent in the British Isles. That these islands have not been mentioned so far is due to the paucity of data available. There does not exist in a public form a national survey which in detail examines the extent and consequences of fragmentation of farm holdings. Stamp[27] refers to the matter but briefly, mentioning the way in which the cultivation of the further fields is influenced by distance from the farmstead. A few local investigations have shown that in some areas the degree of fragmentation is quite serious, as on the Monmouth Moors, around Yetminster, in the Evesham area and in Kent, and it may be inferred that in fact the problem is a widespread one.

Turning our attention away from Europe, we find that in Africa

there are numerous well-attested cases in which the spatial distribution of crops around a village is primarily related to distance
therefrom. Typical of many such villages in west Africa is Soba, in
northern Nigeria.[28] There, four important categories of land use may
be distinguished. Within the village walls, the dwellings are inter-
mingled with 'gardens' where vegetables, culinary herbs and the like
are grown in great profusion and apparent confusion, with close
interplanting and careful catch-cropping. Such 'gardens' require
frequent visits, if only to pluck produce for the next meal, and they
receive manure to enable cultivation to proceed year in and year
out. Outside the walls, continuously cropped land extends to a distance of 0·8–1·2 kilometres, fertilized with manure and the droppings
of the migrant cattle which are kraaled there, growing the staple
crops of Guinea corn, cotton, tobacco and groundnuts. Beyond that
again is a zone varying in width from 0·8 to 1·6 kilometres which is
under rotation farming, the land being cultivated for three to four
years and then allowed to revert to bush for at least five years, to
restore the fertility which would otherwise be entirely destroyed in
the absence of manure. Fourth comes the heavy bush in which there
are small clearings around isolated settlements, these clearings re-
producing the sequence described above. From the account given by
Prothero, it is evident that this general arrangement arises from the
problems posed by distance, though the quality of the terrain modifies
the theoretical symmetry.

A similar situation has been observed in Ghana. Writing of the
village of Agogo, situated east of Kumasi and possessing a population of 4,500 in 1946, Steel observed:

the clear distinction between the area within a mile or so of the town,
where are most of the food-farms, and the zone beyond which is mainly
under cocoa. This is partly to be explained by the ecological conditions,
and partly by the fact that food farms need to be visited at frequent
intervals throughout the year while cocoa once established needs very
little attention, no more than an occasional weeding between the trees
and the plucking of the pods when ripe.[29]

The same type of thing has been recorded as occurring in the
French-speaking territories of Africa, in Senegal for example, where
cotton, cassava and millet are found near the villages and fallow,
groundnuts and millet at a further remove. Or it may be that garden
crops, maize, millet, cotton, tobacco and groundnuts are found near

at hand in a system of polyculture, and millet further away as extensive monoculture merging into the bush.[30]

Much the same account also comes from Uttar Pradesh in India:

The most fertile, heavily manured, and irrigated land surrounds the village. Beyond this lies another zone given over to the chief food crops and irrigated from wells or canals. An outermost zone, the poorest in fertility, is used for dry cultivation, usually millets and fodder crops. (This pattern is replaced in the eastern districts by one in which the outermost block of land is low-lying and wet, and is used for paddy) ... Residing in the central cluster [of houses], the villager is at a minimum economic distance from his scattered fields.[31]

It would be tedious to continue the catalogue further, for the evidence already quoted is ample to prove that the zoning of production around villages in accordance with the principles of von Thünen is a common and widespread phenomenon. The reader who is nevertheless not convinced may wish to consult the remarkable compilation of material published by Sautter,[32] who arrived at very similar conclusions by inductive means and apparently without reference to the deductive system of location theory.

Arising from the above analysis, two further points deserve attention. Doubtless it has already occurred to the reader that some of the cases which have been cited are examples of a system which is often called infield-outfield that was common in much of western Europe throughout the Middle Ages and later, but more particularly characteristic of the Celtic regions of the western littoral and uplands. As the very name indicates, this was an agricultural system built upon two foundations: the infield was that land near the dwellings which was in continuous cultivation year after year; the outfield was the territory which lay further off and though subject to the plough was given periodic respite. Though much the same crops might be grown on both the infield and the outfield, the former received manure, whereas the latter had to rely upon periods of fallow to restore its fertility. Essentially, this was a system providing two levels of intensity of arable use, with a third zone of more extensive exploitation as grazing lying beyond. In Yorkshire, the nearer 'part of the township commanded a higher rent than land in the outfield and was also preferred to other parts of the open fields when new crops came to be introduced.'[33] This pattern is clearly in conformity with von Thünen's ideas, though much influenced by the inherent qualities of the terrain.

So far, the discussion has been conducted with an implicit assumption that the settlements are permanent and immovable. For many peoples, scattered throughout much of Africa, parts of South America and Australasia, a single abode may not be inhabited above five or six years before another site is selected and another home created. Within this system of shifting cultivation, the problems of distance have their impact in a manner which is every bit as forceful as in the case of permanent settlements. The Azande people have been closely studied by de Schlippé,[34] who came to the following conclusions. In selecting a new site, the Azande invariably choose to build their home on the most fertile type of soil which forms one band in the catena that rises from the valley floor to the crest of the interfluve. Once the settlement is established, two types of land use quickly develop. The first is immediately adjacent to the homestead and consists of the permanent cultivation of a *mélange* of crops, with the application of manures and garbage to maintain fertility. Beyond this zone, which is confined to the fertile band of the soil catena, a more extensive system prevails—in all directions and, therefore, on the more fertile soil as well as the less bountiful. The bush is cleared annually, cassava, millet and other crops are planted, and the land may then be allowed to revert to bush or it may be cleared for another crop. From the maps de Schlippé compiled showing the areas actually cultivated each year, it is readily apparent that the following pattern exists. Immediately beyond the zone which is continuously cultivated, the land is in fact put under crops practically every year. As the distance from the homestead increases, the frequency with which the same plot is cleared diminishes, until it may be sown only once. Although there is no change in the type of crop being grown, the intensity of land use steadily diminishes in all directions.

As time passes, the unfertilized lands which are nearest the homestead become exhausted and cultivation must be pushed ever further afield, with the consequence that the cost of cultivation—as measured by the amount of labour required to produce a given quantity of goods—rises. The point comes when it is worth while to remove the whole household to a new site, since the cost of resettling will be fully compensated by the saving in cultivation costs. Hence, the rational nature of shifting cultivation and the fact that it displays certain characteristics which are readily explicable in terms of location principles.

Shifting cultivation displays in an extreme form a principle of widespread importance: while the further lands are unused or under-used, the nearer are exploited beyond the limits they are able to sustain indefinitely. In the case of shifting cultivators, the settlement traditionally moves before the results become serious. In other parts of the world, where the cultivators are sedentary, soil exhaustion, leading to erosion, may become a real menace on the nearer lands, threatening the whole economy of the settlement. Degradation of the land has occurred around such cities as Kampala, Kano, Singapore and St Vincent.[35] The East African Royal Commission[36] discovered that, under conditions of head porterage, the cultivation of maize near coastal villages had resulted in serious damage, while bush remained uncleared further away on account of the transport costs.

Under conditions of extreme fragmentation giving rise to considerable distances between the plots and farmsteads, some of the worse effects which have been discussed above may be avoided in the following manner. One peasant may let some of his further plots to another, from whose farmstead the plots are more accessible. The first peasant may then rent some land on the same basis, either from his partner in the first transaction or from some third party. In this way, although the pattern of *ownership* means that some parcels are far removed from the farmsteads, the pattern of *operation* is rather less unfavourable. A particular case of this is found in Almeria, Spain,[37] but the practice is also widespread over much of Europe, including Britain and Asia.

The basis of the argument in this chapter has been the proposition that human labour is scarce, and that human energies may be bent upon several alternative ends. From this position it has been argued that an attempt will be made to equate the cost of the last dose of labour with the benefits which accrue from it. Now it is commonly held that this fundamental assumption ceases to be valid in circumstances where labour is unemployed or under-employed; human time saved in one process of cultivation adds nothing to the general welfare, there being no productive use to which it can be put. If this were so, no kind of zoning would be apparent, because all the territory would be farmed to the same level of intensity.

An individual peasant, operating his own land, may have one member of his family unemployed. It will then be worth while to raise the general level of intensity of land use much above that level which would otherwise prevail, since every small addition to the total product is clear gain in economic terms. However, poverty is relative to what one is accustomed to receive and one's ideas about what is right, and the point will be reached when it is preferable to sit in the shade and have social intercourse than to toil in the sun for a pittance. But more important, whatever the general level of intensity achieved, it will still remain advantageous to obtain an equal marginal return from the marginal input on each plot, since otherwise production could be raised with no increase in labour merely by a spatial readjustment of the level of inputs. Thus it will still be desirable to arrange the spatial pattern of production in accordance with the principles we have been propounding, though the general level of intensity will be higher than under conditions of full employment, where there are alternative occupations.

Where there is unemployment, the same will be true of hired labour, which may receive only a pittance for a day's work. For the person who hires the workers it is clearly desirable that the amount of time actually spent at work and not travelling should be as great as possible, which puts a premium upon the more intensive use of the nearer land.

Where the unemployment is seasonal and not continued throughout the year, the argument presented in this chapter also remains intact. The farming system will be geared to the availability of labour at the times of peak demand—usually at seeding and harvest times—when there may actually be a shortage of manpower. The disposition of land uses will be adjusted to this situation of seasonably scarce labour.

In this context it is worth noting that in southern Italy, Sicily, Sardinia and Spain there is a great deal of rural unemployment—indeed, in this respect these areas are notorious. However, the spatial zoning of cultivation is here more strikingly apparent than in most of the rest of Europe. We may conclude, therefore, that in fact the relative spatial disposition of land uses will not be affected by the existence of unemployment or under-employment.

To end this chapter, it will be useful to summarize very briefly the conclusions which emerge. It is quite apparent that the problem of distance is sufficiently great for there to be a response in the patterns of land use on farms and around villages in all parts of the world, as a common phenomenon. We have also been able to gain some idea of the magnitude of the effect upon gross and net production. The Finnish data, for example, showed a very rapid diminution with distance, while the Dutch and Pakistani material displayed a somewhat less precipitate decline. In view of the difficulty of working

c

with the kind of material which is available, this difference need cause no surprise. All these studies agree in showing that at a distance of 1 kilometre the decline in net return is large enough to be significant as a factor adversely affecting the prosperity of the farming population, and this order of magnitude corresponds with the opinions quoted by Dovring. These quantitative data on money returns indicate that, at about 3–4 kilometres, the costs of operation rise sufficiently to be oppressive and seriously detrimental, and in general the descriptive material quoted tends to confirm that it is exceptional for distances greatly to exceed this limit with any frequency. The matter will be taken up again in Chapter 7, where, on the basis of the material which has been presented, an attempt will be made to measure some of the economic costs attributable to different degrees of nucleation of rural settlement.

BIBLIOGRAPHICAL NOTES

1. 'The consolidation of farms in six countries of Western Europe', *International Journal of Agrarian Affairs*, May 1952, p. 18.

2. Private communication from Prof. E. W. Hofstee. See maps 10 and 11 in his book *Rural Life and Rural Welfare in the Netherlands*, 1957.

3. F. Dovring, *Land and Labour in Europe in the Twentieth Century*, 3rd edition, 1965, p. 41.

4. J. L. Buck, *Land Utilization in China*, 1937, p. 183.

5. R. N. Khan, *Survey of Small Holdings in the Punjab*, Board of Economic Enquiry, Punjab (Pakistan), 1955, p. 8.

6. J. T. P. Bijhouwer, 'Kavelmaten hier en elders', *Landbouwkundig Tijdschrift*, 1949, pp. 18–20.

7. R. C. Harris, *The Seigneurial System in Early Canada: A Geographical Study*, 1966.

8. A. Meynier, *Les Paysages Agraires*, 1958, pp. 117–18.

9. W. Müller-Wille, *Die Ackerfluren in Landesteil Birkenfeld* (dissertation), Bonn, 1936. His map is reproduced by Lösch, 1954, *supra* (ch. 1), p. 382.

10. J. Piel-Desruisseaux, *Cours d'Organisation Scientifique du Travail en Agriculture*, Institut d'Organisation Scientifique du Travail en Agriculture, mimeographed lecture notes, p. v–2.

11. *The Times*, 24 November 1962: F. Coolman and H. Willems, 'Mechanization and the small farm', in J. L. Meij (Ed.), *Mechanization in Agriculture*, 1960, p. 296: A. Martin, *The Oil Palm Economy of The Ibibio Farmer*, 1956, p. 25.

12. A. Wiiala, *Uusjaon Vaikutuksesta Jakokunnau Maatalousteen*, 1948.

13. T. J. Virri, 'Maanjako-olojen Vaikutuksesta Maataloustuotantous', *Maatalous Agronomien Yhdistkysen Julkaisa*, 1946, pp. 6–11.

14. S. Suomela, 'Peltojen Sijainnin Vaikutuksesta Maatilan Talouteen', *Acta Agralia Fennica*, No. 71, 1950, p. 146. ('On the influence of the location of fields on farming', with an English summary. A brief summary is contained in *International Journal of Agrarian Affairs*, 1952, *supra*, pp. 18–22.)

15. G. Larsson, *Inflyandet ar Avståndet från Bruckningscentrum till Inagojorden på Arbetsbehov, Driftsformer och Driftsresultat*, 1947. (*The influence of the distance between the farm centre and the farm land upon the need of work, the kind of farming and the economical (sic) result*, with a summary in English.)

16. W. C. Visser, 'Gedachten en Getallen over de Geldelijke Gevolgen van Ruilverkalen', *Landbouwkundig Tijdschrift*, 1950, pp. 993–1,010.

17. A. P. Takes, *Physical Planning in Connection with Land Reclamation and Improvement*, International Institute for Land Reclamation and Improvement, 1958, p. 28.

18. Khan, 1955, *supra*, p. 8.

19. Visser, 1950, *supra*.

20. M. Draisma, *Teelt en Bemesting op Bouwland in de Practijk*, Ministerie van Landbouw, 1958, p. 113. (*Cultivation and fertilisation of field crops as practiced (sic) in the Netherlands*, with an English summary.)

21. N. Prestianni, *L'Economia Agraria delle Sicilia*, 1947, pp. 98–9.

22. M. le Lannou, *Pâtres et Paysans de la Sardaigne*, 1941, p. 188.

23. P. Birot, J. Dresch, *La Méditerranée et le Moyen-Orient*, Vol. I, 1953, p. 218.

24. B. B. Pons, 'Evolucion de la estructura agraria del Termino de Ocaña', *Estudios Geograficos*, 1956, pp. 190–1.

25. Birot and Dresch, 1953, *supra*, p. 83.

26. E. de Laveleye, *De la Propriété et ses Formes Primitives*, 5th edn., 1901, p. 12.

27. L. D. Stamp, *The Land of Britain: its Use and Misuse*, 1948.

28. R. M. Prothero, 'Land use at Soba, Zaria Province, Northern Nigeria', *Economic Geography*, 1957, pp. 72–86.

29. R. W. Steel, 'Ashanti Survey, 1945–46: an experiment in social research', *Geographical Journal*, 1947, Vol. CX, p. 159.

30. P. Pélissier, 'Les paysans sérères: essai sur la formation d'un terroir du Sénégal', *Les Cahiers d'Outre-Mer*, 1953, pp. 105–27; J. Dubourg, 'La vie des paysans Mossi: le village de Taghella', *Les Cahiers d'Outre-Mer*, 1957, pp. 285–324.

31. E. Ahmad, 'Rural settlement types in the Uttar Pradesh (United Provinces of Agra and Oudh)', *Annals*, Association of American Geographers, 1952, p. 232.

32. G. Sautter, 'A propos de quelques terroirs d'Afrique occidentale: essai comparatif', *Études Rurales*, 1962, pp. 24–86.

33. A. Harris, *The Rural Landscape of the East Riding of Yorkshire, 1700–1850*, 1961, p. 25.

34. P. de Schlippé, *Shifting Cultivation in Africa: the Zande System of Agriculture*, 1956.

35. Verbal communication from G. B. Masefield, Oxford.

36. East Africa Royal Commission, *Report*, Cmd. 9475, 1955, p. 120.

37. S. Llobet, 'Utilizaccion del suelo y economia del agua en la region semiarida de Huercal-Overa (Almeria)', *Estudios Geograficos*, 1958, pp. 13–14.

5

THE REGION AND THE WORLD: I

At the small scale of phenomenon—the farm and village—it was noted that the cost of overcoming distance arises largely, if not exclusively, from the amount of human time expended, both in accompanying all inputs and produce and in transferring from one site of operations to another. Therefore, it is possible to measure costs directly in terms of man-hours, or if preferred these may be converted into monetary costs. With the larger scales of location, the costs caused by distance are expressed directly in cash terms and, in the present context, pertain much more to the movement of goods than to persons. Transport services may be obtained from private or public companies for a cash payment, or they may be provided by the firm itself. In the latter case a monetary outlay is necessary to purchase, maintain and run the vehicles, and so transport costs are measured directly in cash terms.

Though cost is the main consideration, time does still have considerable importance. Many agricultural products are highly perishable: either they must be marketed within relatively few hours of being uprooted, or preservative devices must be applied to prolong the life of the fruits, meat or dairy produce. The most important of these devices is refrigeration, for which new applications continue to be found; a recent example is the success attaching to experiments in the refrigerated transport of watercress.[1] Increasingly significant is the use of inert gases, as in the preservation of dessert apples. However, these techniques add to the cost of transport by simultaneously raising the capital outlay on rolling stock (or ships) and terminal facilities and reducing the useful load which may be carried.

In the absence of such precautions, the costs imposed by time are measurable in terms of the deterioration of the produce, with high wastage and lower unit value.

Some indication of the importance which does attach to time in the transport of perishable goods is given by the following figures, which relate to railway traffic in 1933:

TABLE 8

U.S.A., 1933: DISTANCE TRAVELLED PER DAY IN TRANSIT, LOADING, UNLOADING AND DELAYS INCLUDED

Commodity	Kilometres	Commodity	Kilometres
Live animals	303	Petroleum	98
Perishables	256	Forest products	92
Appliances	192	Bulk grain	61
Iron and steel	167	Coal and coke	53
		Sand and gravel	43

Source: M. Beckmann, C. B. McGuire, C. B. Winsten, *Studies in the Economics of Transportation*, 1956, p. 116.

Otherwise, time as such only engages our attention in general terms. Insurance rates in transit are greater than in store, so that the longer a commodity is in movement the greater the costs incurred on that account. The more rapidly a vehicle travels, the greater is its productivity in terms of ton-kilometres or passenger-kilometres, and this is one factor affecting the level of charges. Productivity calculations are a favourite pastime of airline and shipping companies, often being crucial to the profitability of the enterprise. These considerations and others relating to time are reflected in the level of charges levied upon goods and passengers and need not be considered separately.

It is of fundamental importance to distinguish between the charge which is levied for a transport service and the costs which are involved in providing that service. There is no necessary relationship, as is apparent from any of the standard textbooks on the economics of transport.[2] That which is charged by the transport company is a cost to the firm consigning the goods and in the discusssion which follows the term 'cost' will be used in this sense. After all, our decisions about the use of transport facilities are based on what it costs *us*, and not upon an estimate of the expenses incurred by the transport company. A recent example illustrating this point is the reduction of railway rates on grain consigned from Chicago and elsewhere to ports on the eastern littoral of the United States. The reason lies not in a decline in railway operating expenses, but in the opening to traffic in 1959 of the St Lawrence Seaway, a competing medium of transport offering lower rates than formerly obtained on the railways.

A second difference distinguishing the smaller and larger scales of phenomena is that the point to which produce is taken ceases generally to be the same spot from which the inputs emanate. For example, the sugar beet of East Anglian farmers is sent to the factories of the British Sugar Corporation, but fertilizers, animal feeds and machinery are bought from dealers in other locations. Or New Zealand buys most of her agricultural machinery imports from the United Kingdom and western Europe while selling an increasing proportion of her farm products to the Asiatic countries. Hence, the response to distance arising from the marketing of produce will give rise to a pattern related to one set of points, while the pattern related to inputs is based upon another set of points. The resultant organization is therefore vastly more complex than in the smaller scales already discussed, though in principle this same problem obtrudes there too, but, as we have seen, it is of minor importance.

A further consideration is the sheer size of many conurbations, whether London or Tokio. These extensive urban areas constitute the main destinations of much agricultural produce and the source of many farming requisites, such as machinery. Clearly we cannot assume these conurbations to be mere points without some justification. In the previous chapter, it was argued that a village may justifiably be regarded as a point because it is of small area in comparison with the territory surrounding it. Likewise, when contemplating the major urban areas, these can only be treated as points for the purposes of our study if a sufficiently sizable section of the world, or the whole globe, is taken into account. Even the largest conurbations then dwindle into insignificant little blobs. A case will make this clearer. Viewed from London, the coast of Europe is dotted with many ports, to each of which a distinct freight rate prevails on any particular commodity. Each port—whether Rotterdam or Hamburg —has its own unique space-relationships within the European scene. Looked at from New Zealand or Australia by an exporter of butter or meat, these differences become of negligible importance; in fact, it is normal for the shipping companies to quote rates which are identical for all the ports of north-west Europe. For practical purposes, therefore, this part of the world coalesces to form a single minute area which may justifiably be regarded as a point when considering certain aspects of international trade and world production patterns.

When dealing with large regions, or the whole world, a vast range of geological, topographical, climatic and political conditions is brought within our purview. For this reason, it were foolish to expect the single factor of distance—which is not even geographical distance but is economic distance, related to transport charges—to account for all phenomena, or even always to provide readily discernible regularities. The purpose of the rest of this chapter is to show how, within the milieu of physical environment and political circumstances, the problem of overcoming distance does confer a good deal of logic to spatial distributions. A beginning will be made with a simple situation, the existence of a single line of communication through a territory and the patterns of land use which develop as a consequence; thereafter, attention will be directed towards the large urban agglomerations, taking the case of the United Kingdom as an example.

A single transport route

When considering a single line of overland communication, it must be remembered that access to it is not always possible at all points. This is particularly the case with railways, where access is only to be had at the stations, which commonly have a settlement in the vicinity. But the same thing is true in greater or lesser degree of canals, rivers and roads, and hence such a route may in the literal sense be considered as a string of beads, each bead representing a point of access and commonly, but not necessarily, a settlement. For practical purposes, the 'beads' are usually near enough together for the route to be treated as approximating a continuous line.

One of the better-documented examples comes from north America at the time of European colonization in the prairies. Apart from railways, overland transport was conducted by horse and cart, which severely restricted the distance over which it was economic to transport wheat from the farm to the station. Mackintosh[3] devoted a chapter to the relationship between the pattern of settlement and the construction of railways in the Canadian prairies, from which certain main conclusions emerge. New settlement for agricultural purposes was mostly confined to land within reach of an existing railway, or near the alignment of a projected or anticipated route. Thus, while it was common for settlers to cart their wheat as much as 80 kilometres, this was only done in the expectation that subsequent railway construction would reduce the haul to railhead to between 16 and 24 kilometres at the most. Greater distances were found not to be economic on a long-term basis and consequently the railway companies found it advantageous to construct a network sufficiently dense for most land to be contained within belts extending to 16 kilometres on either hand. Where the distance remained permanently greater than this, the cost of wagon carriage of wheat rendered it unprofitable to market and it was common for farmers so situated to convert the grain into livestock, which, being able to walk, could better support the cost of transport to railhead.

The same phenomenon has been described in Australia, where in the wheat belt railways now generally serve a territory extending about 24 kilometres on either side. During the 1890's, the economic limit of haul to the nearest station varied according to the price received by the farmers for their wheat: at a price of 3s. or 2s. 9d. a bushel, it was scarcely worth growing grain even under 16 kilometres from the railway, but with a price of 4s. 8d. the tributary zone extended to nearly 50 kilometres.[4] Grazing occupied the more distant lands.

An interesting case is found in English history, relating to the supply of timber and having important repercussions on the course of economic and military affairs. Before the advent of iron, steel and concrete, timber was a universally important construction material, alike for ships and houses; before coal and coke came into general use, wood and charcoal were the chief fuels. During the sixteenth and seventeenth centuries, the rate of consumption outstripped the supply available from home resources and shortages of all types of timber became acute. Writing of ship timber, Albion observed that:

when the period of shortage came, there was still plenty of good oak in England, but much of it was inaccessible. Twenty miles [32 kilometres] was ordinarily considered a maximum [overland] haul. Beyond that distance land carriage added heavily to the cost of timber, so that in the more remote localities many great oaks which would have made splendid ship timber were cut up for ordinary carpenter's purposes. The strips of woodland within fifteen or twenty miles [24–32 kilometres] of the coast or navigable rivers were the first places to be exploited for timber.[5]

The significance of this problem of overland transport for timber can easily be appreciated from the maps which Willan[6] has prepared, showing those areas of England and Wales situated more than 24 kilometres from navigable waters at various dates. Considerable tracts of southern England, where grew the finest ship timber, and much of the central and northern portions of the country were at a greater remove from passable waters and therefore were under-exploited or neglected entirely except to supply local needs. Confirmation of the point is found in an Act early in the reign of Elizabeth I forbidding iron workers to use trees of more than 0·3 of a metre in diameter within 22 kilometres of the sea; but this was not successful in its object, namely the preservation of timber supplies for ship construction.

Domestic supplies could have been enlarged, at least for a limited period, by exploiting forests even further removed from water transport, but the costs became too great. Sea-coal came to replace wood and charcoal as a fuel, iron smelting shifted in location to areas of more abundant charcoal supplies, bricks and stone replaced the timber frame hitherto characteristic of dwelling-houses, timbers other than oak were sought as substitutes and imports became increasingly important. While the zone of timber supply could be measured in tens of kilometres over land and failed to include the whole domestic territory, by sea the radius of supply extended hundreds of kilometres to embrace Scandinavia and western Russia, the western maritime regions of North America and even New Zealand. The commercial policies adopted by successive sovereigns and the political manœuvres related to these policies were continuously framed with reference to the need to ensure economically priced supplies of timber, especially for shipbuilding, until after the Napoleonic wars.

But is it not so that this simple form of zoning around single lines of communication is a thing of the past, of historical interest only? Of its very nature, this phenomenon is likely to be transient, as an economy evolves and a more complicated network of routes is developed. In north America and Australia, the railway network rapidly became dense enough for most land in the fertile areas to be economically accessible to a station and the elementary zoning related to individual routes ceased to be discernible over most of the territory. This occurred even before the advent of modern motor transport. In the case of the English forests, river improvement and the construction of canals and railways resulted in a multiplication of routes capable of handling bulky timber and made possible the exploitation of even remote forests, destroying the relatively simple pattern of zoning. Under these circumstances, regional zoning of land use in relation to single lines of communication becomes progressively less important: but at the same time greater significance attaches to the converse proposition—given the existing pattern of economic development, what alignment should be chosen for a new route? To this problem we shall turn in Chapter 8.

But two aspects of the matter merit further discussion. First, in highly developed countries we can still see some aspects of zoning related to individual routes, in the form of land values on either hand and the consequent adjustments in land use. In the United States, it is a popular exercise, when considering the prospective benefits to be conferred by a new or improved road, to allow for increases in land values on adjacent properties. Concomitant with such rises will be changes of use, frequently from agricultural to urban uses. The visible evidence of this may be seen in many American cities and almost universally in the United Kingdom—ribbon development of residental and industrial properties along roads radiating from, encircling or by-passing towns.[7] Such increases in value and induced change of use consequent upon new road construction are an example of one of the considerations underlying the 1947 Town and Country Planning Act of Britain's first post-war Labour government; society, it was felt, had a right to reap the full benefit of any property values which were created by corporate acts. Whether just or not, it proved to be too complicated to administer and the development charges part of the Act was subsequently rescinded, later to be replaced by the 1967 Act which set up the Land Commission.

Second, large tracts of the world are still at an early stage in the process of economic development. Much of Africa, south and central America, large areas of Asia, Borneo and New Guinea have never witnessed modern forms of transport, or possess but rudimentary networks. Here are ideal conditions in which zoning about single lines of communication can and does occur. It will be many decades before such economies become sufficiently complex and developed for the simple zoning to disappear. Of the numerous examples it will suffice to quote only a few, ample to establish the point.

A very well documented case is that of the railway which runs from Port Franqui on the river Kasai, a tributary of the Congo, to the Katanga Province of the former Belgian Congo. Nicolaï and Jacques, in their study of this 1,100-kilometre route,[8] noted that whereas in the 1920's, when the route was built, many of the regions through which it passes were empty of people or but sparsely inhabited, in 1951 some 23 per cent of the population in the administrative areas traversed lived in but 5 per cent of the land area in a belt extending only 2·5 kilometres on either side of the railway. Examining the reasons for this change in the distribution of population, they conclude that it is largely due to immigration into the zone adjacent to the railway:

It is undeniable that the narrow strip which borders the railway has experienced growth of population, by the establishment of numerous villages peopled by immigrants . . . and by the development of a series of urban centres . . . where absolutely no important towns existed before 1922.[9]

Many of the immigrants were labourers who worked on the railway and then chose to settle locally instead of returning home. An important attraction was the possibility of engaging in commercial agriculture for sale. The result has been the development of alimentary crops—notably cassava—for sale in the mining areas of Katanga and of crops such as cotton and more recently rubber and coffee for export abroad. The prices of these products decline with distance from the railway, as is illustrated by the case of manioc in the Kasai region:

Distance from railway in kms.	*Price in francs per kilogramme*
Up to 15	1·5
15–30	1·45
90–105	1·2
105–120	1·15
135–150	1·05
Over 150	1·00

The foodcrops are relatively bulky and of low unit value and so derive the greatest advantage from being near the transport artery. Hence, there is an inner zone of these crops—where, incidentally, farms are very small—and the cotton cultivation is found further away. As a result of the growth of population and the expansion of cash sales in conjunction with static agricultural techniques, severe degradation of the soil is taking place in the most favourably located areas which are the most intensively used, while the remoter parts remain in forest.

After the last world war Ecuador was not an important producer of bananas, but has now become the world's leading exporter. Most of the plantations have been established where hitherto the forest reigned supreme, on land which has only recently been made accessible to modern means of transport. 'Wherever conditions permit, banana farms line these new travel arteries.'[10] Beyond this strip of farmed territory lies the undisturbed forest, where transport costs are too high to permit of cultivation. A similar situation is common in Ghana, where the construction of modern transport facilities has resulted in the land-use pattern taking on a 'ribbon-like appearance, the zones of cultivation [being] aligned along the roads.'[11] Of British Guiana we are vouchsafed the following description:

> Modernisation of the road [from Georgetown] to Atkinson airport is a striking proof of the principle in colonial development, that if you drive a road or railway through a cultivatable [sic] area you automatically stimulate economic development. Ten years ago this was a dismal track 23 miles [37 kilometres] long, running through neglected savannah and flanked by the odd peasant's shack. The British troops who came in at the time of the 1953 emergency saw this as their first view of British Guiana, and were sorely troubled by the experience. Today the road has been widened and macadamised.
>
> What is more remarkable, however, is the ribbon development which has followed. There are habitations, many of them prosperous looking, all the way. Alongside the Colonial Development Corporation's saw-mill, now a paying concern, have sprung up a beer factory and a margarine factory, and along the road ground is being cultivated which was not cultivated before, and small concerns like chicken farms have taken root.[12]

As a final point before turning to larger scales of consideration, notice that in the present day development does take place in anti-cipation of the construction of routes, repeating events already noted in the American and Canadian plains. A deliberately planned case of this is occurring in the state of São Paulo, Brazil, with the extension of the road and rail network into the interior.[13] The East African Royal Commission noticed that spontaneous agricultural development by Africans had occurred ahead of the construction of a road inland from the coast, on territory which previously was neglected on account of the high costs of head porterage.[14]

United Kingdom

In considering the more complicated regional and world patterns, it is helpful to direct attention in some detail to a particular case, and then to show that what is true in one instance also holds more generally. For this purpose, the United Kingdom has been chosen.

We shall begin with a brief study of the development of land use around the city of London up to the advent of the railways, go on to discuss the horticultural and dairying industries during the nineteenth and twentieth centuries and then examine the present-day structure of imports of horticultural and dairy goods. Finally, there will be a few words on other elements of the agricultural economy at the present time.

The story may begin with the century 1540–1640, which has been documented by Fisher.[15] At the end of the sixteenth century, London's food supplies came almost exclusively from a few adjoining shires. 'But as the years pass it is possible to watch the city's tentacles spreading over the provinces until by the middle of the seventeenth century they reached to Berwick, Cornwall and Wales.' Kent was the great granary of London early in the period, but to an increasing extent fruit and vegetable cultivation invaded this and other areas bordering the city, while grain supplies were drawn from further afield, notably Norfolk. While fresh milk and fresh butter were local produce, cheese and salted butter were increasingly brought from further than Essex and Suffolk, from as far as Durham and Northumberland. The meat trade was organized on a national basis, animals and birds being driven from Wales or the north-west of England, pausing in the hither regions to be fattened for market.

The position outlined above was reflected in the prices for grain; at the end of the seventeenth century, prices were about twenty per cent higher in the metropolitan area than elsewhere[16] and no fundamental change had occurred at the time Defoe[17] wrote in the first quarter of the eighteenth century. A closely related phenomenon was that agricultural wages within thirty-two kilometres of London were higher by about seventy-five per cent than in areas distant 177 kilometres or more.[18] The general pattern of agriculture and related land use dependent upon London remained essentially intact until the time of the Napoleonic wars and later, though modifications were evident, especially during the nineteenth century as the consumption of liquid milk rose.

As even a cursory glance will show, the environs of London comprehend a wide range of natural soil conditions, ranging from intractable clays in Essex and Middlesex to light and fertile loams on some of the river gravels to poor but easily worked land on the exposed chalk. Despite this wide variety, the Reverend Henry Hunter, writing in 1811, 'described the face of the land around the capital in terms of a series of concentric belts, each displaying a measure of unity of farming practice.'[19] Beyond the area of buildings and circumadjacent clay pits, a zone of pasture extended to a distance of several kilometres to the north and further in other directions, especially to the west. This pasture was almost exclusively in the hands of cowkeepers who supplied the metropolis with milk, much of the milk being produced in dairies situated in the city or on its outskirts. Fodder was brought in to these dairies and the nearby pastures were heavily fertilized with manure from the city. Beyond them extended tracts of hay land, the produce being consigned to the capital to sustain the cows and the innumerable horses which provided transport of all kinds. The nearer hay lands were also provided with manure from London, but as the distance from the city increased this practice became less common until arable farming with leys of clover and grass became the dominant form of agricultural enterprise. Cutting across these belts was a strip of market gardens extending westwards along the Thames gravels: in this case there was generally a close association between the nature of the soil and the type of enterprise, although this form of production was not confined to the lands best suited to it, but was also found, for example, on the heavier lands to the north-east. As with the pasture and hither hay land, the horticultural holdings received plentiful inputs of manure carted from the city.

The reasons for this pattern are not far to seek. London represented a sizable market for agricultural produce; communications were not good, with the consequence that carrying foodstuffs more than a few kilometres took much time; and certain kinds of produce were highly perishable. By themselves, these considerations were sufficient to ensure that if Londoners were going to consume any quantities of fresh milk and any of a wide range of fresh fruits and vegetables, these would have to be local produce, coming from as near the capital as possible. But in addition, transport provision within the city depended upon horses, and the fodder, particularly the hay, was too bulky to be transported far overland. The population of horses and stall-fed cattle gave a plentiful supply of street sweepings and manure which had to be removed but which was not worth carting very far. The less perishable foods, such as grain, which were reasonably valuable in relation to their bulk could withstand the cost of transport over considerable distances and were perforce banished from the nearer lands. Livestock were walked to market from as far as Wales, the Pennines and even Scotland; they lost condition on the way, but this was often restored by a short period for fattening somewhere in the Home Counties. Notice, also, that the zones of supply extended further along the east coast than elsewhere, on account of the relatively easy access by sea.

The combination of these circumstances early in the nineteenth century and previously produced a pattern of land use which in essentials was exactly of the kind which von Thünen analysed a few decades later. But that was all a long time ago, and is surely not relevant to the present day. Three points effectively answer this objection:

(1) The ideas of von Thünen have their application in historical studies carried out in the present.

(2) The conditions of transport prevailing in England in 1800 were reasonably good by comparison with the situation found in some other parts of the world today or in the very recent past. But a few years ago, a survey of nearly 2,000 lowland rice farms in the Philippines showed that 31 per cent of the farmers consigned their rice to the local market by non-mechanical overland means—that is, by cart, pack animal, sledge and porter. In Visayas, the proportion was 67 per cent, in Mindanao 74 per cent and in Cagayan as much as 99 per cent.[20] Such a situation is by no means uncommon elsewhere and clearly constrains those who specialize in the production of perishable goods to be near their markets.

(3) As will be shown in the succeeding paragraphs, certain elements of the zoning have survived into the present despite the enormous improvements in transport which have taken place.

With the development of the railways and refrigeration during the last century, and of road transport in this, the distance over which milk may be transported and remain in good condition has increased from mere tens of kilometres to hundreds. This has made possible a great enlargement in the area supplying fresh milk to the urban markets. That such an increase has in fact taken place may be attributed to a variety of factors. The urban population has grown a great deal and with rising living standards the per caput consumption of milk has also increased, the combined effect being to raise demand manifold. Cattle disease in the town dairies of London in the 1860's and licensing of such establishments rendered them less attractive propositions than hitherto, while towards the end of the century the growing import of grain struck a heavy blow at arable farming. Much arable land was turned to pasture to supply the rising demand for liquid milk. At the same time, imports of meat and dairy produce forced many farmers away from the production of butter and cheese to the more lucrative business of fresh milk. So radical has been the transformation of British agriculture as a consequence of these forces that currently about a quarter of the gross farm income derives from milk and milk products (mostly liquid milk). Furthermore, most of the country lies within the supply areas of the major urban concentrations: the zone of liquid milk production has extended to embrace almost the whole country.[21]

In some of the remoter areas, it is only since the 1930's that the production of milk for sale has become substantial. Anglesey is a case in point, where stock rearing has traditionally formed the basis of the economy, seasonally surplus milk being converted to butter. Under the aegis of the Milk Marketing Board, a manufacturing creamery was established in 1934 at Bangor on the mainland, which served to divert much milk from stock rearing to the manufacture of milk products; ten years later, a depot was opened on the mainland for the collection of liquid milk, since when milk surplus to local needs has been sent to Liverpool for liquid consumption.[22]

The pricing policy of the Milk Marketing Board tends to encourage the production of milk for liquid consumption in areas remote from the market. The price received by a producer is reduced by a charge for transport. These charges relate to collection from the farm for delivery to the local depot and to onward consignment to the final market. The charge varies according to the region, and the country is divided into sixteen such areas. But the transport levy does not reflect the true cost of transport very closely and makes no allowance for cost variations within the regions. Conversely, the price which consumers pay is uniform throughout the country, there being no differentiation of retail prices in response to the differing geographical costs of provision. In this way the production of liquid milk in areas far from the markets is encouraged to the relative detriment of output nearer at hand.

Nevertheless, the Milk Marketing Board has had some success in its policy of encouraging that manufacture of dairy products which does take place to be located in the remoter regions, especially where a seasonal surplus of supplies is most marked. This can be seen in Fig. 5, which shows changes between 1938–9 and 1965–6 in the amount of milk used for manufacturing purposes in the eleven administrative regions of the Board. There has been a steady rise in the demand for milk for liquid consumption but nevertheless the amount destined for manufacture has also increased, to about 170 per cent of the 1938–9 level. It is evident that by far the greater part

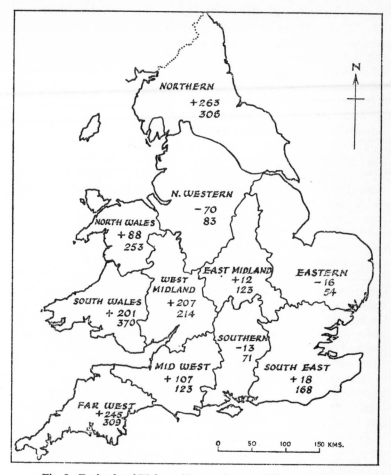

Fig. 5 England and Wales: milk manufacture, 1938–9 and 1965–6. The figures relate to the Milk Marketing Board's regions and show (upper) the absolute change—plus or minus—in the quantity of milk used for manufacture, in million litres, and (lower) 1965–6 as a percentage of 1938–9.

of the increment in milk for manufacture has been in the areas away from the main population concentrations and that indeed there has been an actual decline in milk manufacture in much of England near the big cities. Equally interesting is the fact that in the three

regions which include the Wash, Thames estuary and Southampton
Water, over 85 per cent of the milk used for 'manufacture' goes to
the preparation of fresh cream, whereas the national average is only
20 per cent. Fresh cream is more perishable than butter, cheese,
condensed milk, etc., and therefore tends to be produced near the
main markets, whereas the other products are more prominent in
remoter areas.[23]

As to horticulture, a glance at a land-use map of this country will
show at once that there is a marked concentration of market garden-
ing into certain areas of the country. Broadly speaking, the areas may
be divided into those which are situated adjacent to major urban
areas and those which are located where natural conditions of soil
and climate are peculiarly favourable. Middlesex, Bedfordshire and
Lancashire, for example, contain much horticulture which comes in
the former category, and Lincolnshire and Cornwall that which falls
within the latter. Stated in these terms, where indeed is the influence
of distance?

To answer this question, it is necessary to have a closer look at
the individual crops, for fruits and vegetables are very diverse in
their characteristics and requirements. There is the important anti-
thesis between maincrop products with a long selling season which
command relatively low prices per unit weight and usually also per
hectare, such as turnips and cabbages, and speciality crops with a
limited season which fetch high prices, examples being early potatoes
and asparagus. Then there is also the contrast between the highly
perishable crops and those which remain in good condition for considerable periods after harvesting; lettuces are a case of the former,
lasting barely a few hours after cutting, and onions illustrate
the latter case, keeping for months. Each separate crop
has its own unique combination of characteristics and therefore
analysis of spatial distributions must be concerned with particular
products.

The two broad locational categories of fruit and vegetable growing
mentioned above concentrate on different kinds of produce which
are grown in a different manner. Near the cities, market gardeners
still cultivate the more valuable and perishable crops, such as salad
onions and runner beans, in an intensive manner on comparatively
small holdings. In the case of lettuce, there is little doubt that the

growing areas are so situated in relation to the consuming areas that
only for the produce of about one-third of the area grown in England

and Wales have markets to be found at distances further than approximately 20 miles [32 kilometres].[24]

With lettuce and similar crops, grown either in the open or under glass, the greater part of production is located within one hour's journey time of the main urban centres. In contrast, the cheaper, bulky vegetables, such as parsnips and potatoes, are mostly grown as part of an arable rotation. The individual farmer normally specialises in a few of these crops and grows each on a substantial scale. The intensity of cultivation is lower than on the market gardens and though the crop is of comparatively low value it does not deteriorate quickly and can be handled in large consignments. Hence, crops like carrots or celery may be highly localised in the arable districts—mainly in eastern England—where soils and terrain are suitable. Nevertheless, these crops are all grown within a day's journey of the market.

Table 9 reflects these various considerations as they apply to twenty-seven crops. The coefficient of localisation is the same as Florence[25] used for the analysis of industrial location, except that the area under each crop has been used for the analysis instead of employed persons. The coefficient is obtained by computing the percentage of the total area of each crop in England and Wales found in each county. These percentages are compared with the percentage distribution of the total area of the specified crops. For example, 5·0 per cent of the raspberry acreage is in Worcestershire, whereas this county contains only 3·9 per cent of the total area under the twenty-nine crops. Raspberries deviate from the average by 1·1 percentage points, a positive deviation. All the positive deviations are totalled and the resulting sum divided by 100. If a particular crop were distributed among the counties in a manner identical to the average, the coefficient of localization would be zero. At the other extreme, a value approaching unity indicates a very high degree of localization with respect to the average of the twenty-nine crops. The actual degree of localization is often greater than indicated, for it frequently happens that a very small locality within the county contains that county's total area of the particular crop.

The table shows that the degree of localization of the individual named crops with respect to the aggregate area for all the twenty-seven crops has tended to rise in the post-war period. In 1956, the median coefficient was 0·41 whereas by 1964 it had risen to 0·45; a rather smaller increase is evident if each coefficient is weighted by

TABLE 9

ENGLAND AND WALES, 1956 AND 1964: THE LOCALIZATION OF
OPEN-AIR HORTICULTURAL PRODUCTION,
BASED ON ACREAGE RETURNS

Crop	Coefficient of localisation		Total area, thousand hectares	
	1956	1964	1956	1964
Group 1				
Brussels sprouts	0·48	0·46	19·5	18·1
Carrots	0·45	0·49	13·1	10·5
Peas, green for marketing	0·45	0·47	14·7	8·3
Cauliflower and broccoli	0·38	0·42	10·2	6·7
Peas, green for canning and freezing	0·37	0·33	19·4	32·9
Peas, harvested dry	0·35	0·44	42·5	13·0
Cabbages, savoys, kale and sprouting broccoli	0·20	0·26	22·1	14·7
Group 2				
(a) Celery	0·61	0·56	1·9	2·1
Loganberries and cultivated blackberries	0·60	0·52	0·5	0·4
All bulb flowers not under glass	0·59	0·55	3·5	5·4
Rhubarb	0·58	0·53	2·1	2·3
Tomatoes growing in the open	0·56	0·63	0·4	0·05
(b) Asparagus	0·51	0·54	0·6	0·6
Raspberries	0·46	0·46	1·1	0·6
Blackcurrants	0·44	0·48	4·2	6·4
Red and white currants	0·43	0·48	0·4	0·3
Gooseberries	0·43	0·44	2·3	2·2
Hardy nursery stock	0·41	0·45	5·2	5·8
Strawberries	0·39	0·37	6·8	6·2
Lettuce	0·39	0·43	3·1	3·4
Other flowers, not under glass	0·39	0·39	2·7	2·1
(c) Runner and French beans	0·36	0·36	5·0	7·7
Parsnips	0·33	0·42	2·0	1·8
Turnips and swedes	0·32	0·49	2·2	2·2
Broad beans	0·30	0·26	3·2	4·9
Onions	0·29	0·38	2·3	1·5
Beetroot	0·27	0·33	3·8	3·2
			194·8	163·3

Source: Ministry of Agriculture, *Agricultural Statistics.*

the area under the relevant crop, the weighted mean having increased
from 0·38 to 0·40 in the nine years to 1964. However, these coefficients
of localization are related to the total area devoted to the named
crops and this is also becoming more concentrated geographically.

The coefficient of localization for the total area under the named crops in relation to the whole area of arable land has changed from 0·35 in 1956 to 0·42 in 1964. There has been, therefore, a general and quite rapid increase in the geographical concentration of fruit and vegetable growing in England and Wales, reflecting the decline of many traditional location determinants in favour of other relevant factors.

Following the demise of town dairies from the 1860's and the development of mechanized urban transport during the nineteenth century, the availability of manure supplies from the cities had ceased to be an important location factor early in the twentieth century. On the other hand, the major urban centres continued to be the source of much casual labour, essential for the harvesting of many crops, until after the second world war. Since then, mechanical harvesting devices—for peas, hops, sugarbeet, etc.—have been steadily replacing the gangs of seasonal workers for an ever growing number of crops. Cities have therefore very largely ceased to be important for the supply of two inputs, thereby facilitating the movement of many crops away from the peri-urban areas. However, problems of marketing do still affect many crops, primarily the highly perishable ones like lettuce, and also hardy nursery stock. Much of the latter is grown in scattered locations around but near the main population centres, accessible to the car-owning purchaser who wishes to inspect plants before making his choice. Postal sales on catalogue specifications have not yet seriously modified this pattern.

Other crops have been affected by changes in the manner of marketing, whereby comparatively few merchants now handle most of the sales so that continuity of supply can be ensured and economies of harvesting and selling secured.

Merchants, of whom the number is not large, usually specialise in particular crops or related crops. Chatteris in the Isle of Ely is the centre for the carrot merchants, who may also handle other vegetables such as parsnips and celery, while in the districts around Boston and Wainfleet are those whose main business is in cauliflowers and spring cabbages. . . . For the most part they are themselves substantial growers of the crops they handle. . . . To ensure continuity of supply (an essential part of their business) they may enter into financial arrangements with the smaller growers, usually by agreeing to buy their growing crops by the acre. Moreover, they invariably carry out the harvesting of the crops, having gangs of labour with special experience in this task, and for which the smaller grower is usually ill-provided.[26]

Thus, the production of carrots and other crops is increasingly located near the first point in the marketing chain—the dealer—and is consequently becoming more localized than formerly.

A particularly interesting case is provided by green peas for canning and freezing. Since the mid-1950's, there has been a rapid increase in the area of peas for freezing and with this the construction of numerous factories for processing the peas. It is essential that peas grown for freezing be cultivated to very strict standards and therefore the frozen food companies have to seek out farmers who are able and willing to meet the stringent requirements and who also have land that is suitable. In this situation, expansion of the crop area has been associated with a reduction in the degree of localization but each producing area is closely tied to its 'market,' the processing factory. This tie may become closer in the future. The present practice is for the vines to be harvested mechanically and for the whole plant to be transported to the factory, where the peas are removed from the shells; supplies may reach a factory from up to 64 kilometres. In 1966, a prototype harvester was demonstrated in Britain which not only cuts the vines but combs the peas from the pods at the same time, the peas being transferred to moving lorries which take them to the factory. Since the peas must be frozen within 90 minutes of being shelled, it will not be possible for the crop to be grown very far from the factory.[27]

The distribution of some crops is not as readily explained in the terms that have so far been used. The area around Bedford has long been prominent for Brussels sprouts yet the light sandy soils, especially near Sandy, are not especially suitable for this crop and localization does not appear to have been occasioned by economies in marketing. Nor does there seem to be an adequate explanation for the concentration of rhubarb production near Leeds and of loganberries and cultivated blackberries in Worcestershire and Kent. Nevertheless, when particular crops are viewed in terms of their own characteristics and are related to farming and merchanting systems as a whole, the disorder that appeared at first sight resolves itself into a remarkably rational pattern.

So much for the pattern of milk and horticultural production within this country. It is now time to examine the nature and sources of our imports, beginning with dairy products.

The most striking point to notice is the absence of any imports of liquid milk. It might be claimed that the reason for this lies in our health regulations and the danger of introducing milk-borne diseases, but pasteurization and other techniques are available to meet this difficulty. Nor can it be claimed that the 10 per cent *ad valorem* duty is a sufficient deterrent, as many commodities are purchased abroad despite much heavier duties. Fundamentally, milk is insufficiently valuable in relation to its bulk, and too perishable, for it to be economic to import, despite the fact that many continental producers receive a substantially lower price for their milk than do our farmers. Only under crisis conditions has liquid milk been imported into Great Britain—by air from Northern Ireland. Even when the volume has been reduced to roughly one-third that of the original whole milk, as is the case with condensed milk, the amount imported is not large. Only where the bulk has been reduced to about 10–15 per cent or less do imports become important, as with cream, cheese, butter and dried milk. With this reduction in volume, the keeping qualities are much enhanced.

Thus, the primary pattern of imports conforms to our expectations. But let us look closer at the origins of imports of processed dairy goods. The position is analysed in Table 11 and Fig. 6. Notice that virtually all the fresh cream comes from Zone 1, mostly from Eire, and that the greater part of the preserved cream and condensed milk comes from the same zone. By contrast, cheese, butter and milk powder come from the ends of the earth. These represent the most highly manufactured products, with the greatest loss of weight, to which it is therefore most worth while to apply refrigeration (butter and cheese, not dried milk).

It will be seen that this pattern is consistent with the following approximate figures for the weight of product obtained from one million litres of liquid milk, remembering the perishable nature of cream:

TABLE 10

WEIGHT OF SINGLE PRODUCT OBTAINED FROM
1 MILLION LITRES OF MILK
(*in Metric Tons*)

Butter	39
Cream	82
Cheese	99
Dried milk, full cream	124
Condensed milk, full cream	372

Source: Figures from K. R. Clark, Institute for Research in Agricultural Economics, Oxford.

TABLE 11

UNITED KINGDOM, 1960–2: IMPORTS OF SELECTED
HORTICULTURAL AND DAIRY PRODUCTS
(*by Weight*)

Commodity	Imports as % of gross supplies	% of imports originating from zone:				
		Zone 1	Zone 2	Zone 3	Zone 4	Other countries
Potatoes, not new	0·9	67·0	—	22·8	—	10·2
Cabbages	1·1	93·6	—	—	—	6·4
Strawberries	2·3	4·4	85·7	2·8	—	7·1
Carrots	6·8	25·6	15·0	50·4	—	9·0
Lettuces, endives	9·0	88·1	—	—	—	11·9
Plums	10·8	1·0	72·3	0·4	14·1	12·2
Asparagus	11·1	—	74·6	—	—	25·4
Cherries	11·3	—	94·7	2·8	—	2·5
Cauliflower, broccoli	11·3	2·2	95·9	—	—	1·9
Cucumbers	16·4	82·8	—	14·2	—	3·0
Potatoes, new	29·8	11·9	38·8	44·9	—	4·4
Apples	30·9	2·5	15·8	19·3	61·8	0·6
Pears	52·1	7·1	26·5	5·9	55·8	4·7
Tomatoes	62·8	23·7	16·3	59·7	—	0·3
Onions	90·2	28·8	40·5	19·7	7·6	3·4
Milk, preserved, not dried	−18·8*	96·8	—	—	—	3·2
Cream, fresh	6·8	100·0	—	—	—	—
Milk, powder	30·1	23·9	15·9	—	59·7	0·5
Cream, preserved	43·2	99·3	—	—	—	0·7
Cheese, other than blue-vein	54·3	15·6	2·9	7·4	73·4	0·7
Butter	98·1†	31·0	11·5	—	56·6	0·9

* Net export, mainly to tropical and sub-tropical countries.
† All imports as % of all home production of all cheese types.
Zone 1. Belgium, Channel Islands, Denmark, Eire, Netherlands, Norway.
Zone 2. Austria, Finland, France, Italy, Poland, Spain, Sweden, Switzerland, Yugoslavia.
Zone 3. Algeria, Canada, Canary Islands, Cyprus, Egypt, Lebanon, Libya, Malta, Morocco, United States.
Zone 4. Argentina, Australia, Chile, East Africa, New Zealand, South Africa.
    Sources: Official production and trade returns, with some supplementation from unofficial sources.

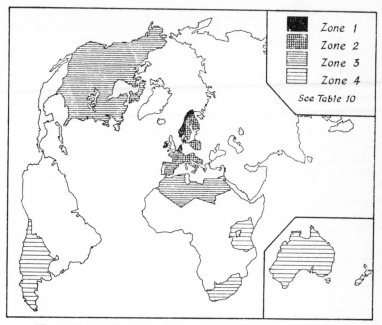

Fig. 6   United Kingdom, 1960–2: imports of selected horticultural and dairy products. Oblique Azimuthal Projection showing distances correct from London.

However, as every housewife knows, Danish butter is a very different commodity from the New Zealand product, with a different flavour and texture, being but lightly salted or unsalted and consequently having much poorer keeping qualities. This difference in quality arises from the measures of preservation which the New Zealand manufacturers and exporters have to take to market their goods. Likewise, our imports of cheese from New Zealand are exclusively of the Cheddar type, which has good keeping qualities, whereas from the Continent come the soft cheeses like Gorgonzola, Camembert and Brie, which are in prime condition for a very short time. Hence, although the global figures reveal much, the detailed situation displays an even more convincing degree of logic.

The pattern of imports of fruits and vegetables displays features similar to those of dairy imports. The items shown in Table 10 are those listed in the foreign trade returns which compete directly with home products. Products which are not grown in this country have been excluded from consideration, though it must be remembered that imports of oranges and bananas, for example, do compete with home-produced apples and plums for the favours of consumers. The distinction which has been chosen is arbitrary but convenient and the argument would not be affected by the inclusion of those crops which are omitted from the analysis; it would only be made longer and more complicated.

A point of fundamental importance in the analysis of the import trade in fruits and vegetables is the seasonality of supplies. The same consideration does apply to dairy imports but is much less important and so can be ignored in the present context. With fruits and vegetables, the matter is well illustrated by the case of potatoes. In a normal year, the production of maincrop varieties suffices for virtually all our ware potato requirements with but small supplementary imports, mainly from Belgium and the Netherlands. But home-produced new potatoes do not begin to come on to the market until the year is well advanced; especially in the months of April, May and June the gap is filled by imports. Table 12 sets out the relevant

TABLE 12

UNITED KINGDOM, 1962: IMPORTS OF NEW POTATOES, FEBRUARY–JULY

(Percentage of imports, by weight)

Country of origin	February	March	April	May	June	July
Belgium	—	—	—	0·5	0·5	16·7
Greece	—	—	—	3·9	4·2	7·7
Egypt	—	2·8	2·1	11·7	1·4	16·3
France	—	—	—	0·2	6·5	0·2
Netherlands	—	—	—	5·0	6·0	3·0
Cyprus	24·6	14·2	2·9	10·6	40·4	16·4
Italy	2·3	0·3	5·1	13·1	31·1	11·9
Malta and Gozo	—	—	1·5	2·9	0·6	—
Spain	1·3	21·0	37·4	39·9	—	—
Canary Is.	22·3	27·2	37·5	5·9	0·7	—
Morocco	49·5	29·8	12·7	0·7	1·6	0·5
Others	—	4·7	0·8	5·6	7·0	27·3
Total	100·0	100·0	100·0	100·0	100·0	100·0
Total imports, metric tons:	*February*	*March*	*April*	*May*	*June*	*July*
	11,360	36,340	37,000	113,710	120,150	41,050

Source: Potato Marketing Board, *Report on the Operation of the Potato Marketing Scheme*, year ended 30 June 1962, p. 61. 1962 is the last year for which the Board published these data.

information for 1962. It will be seen at once that the eleven countries listed may be separated into three major divisions: the Canary Islands and Morocco have a clear advantage in the early months of the year, Belgium and the Netherlands in July. The pattern of exports from the remaining countries is less clear-cut. The greater period over which these countries send their major contributions may be due to the variety of physical conditions found within their borders, which attribute is particularly striking for Italy. Indeed, Italy clearly displays within her own confines the principle which underlies the seasonal distribution of the sources of our new potato imports: as the season advances the demand for supplies can be met by lands lying progressively further north and nearer the destination of the consignments. Like a concertina, the supply area expands and contracts, according to the season.

Turnips and swedes are regarded as inferior vegetables for which only a low price is paid and because they are bulky they are not imported. Cabbages are a bulky, perishable and cheap vegetable for which the demand does at times rise high enough to warrant imports, but virtually all of these come from the Netherlands. Rather superior articles are cauliflowers and heading broccoli, the production of which is seasonal; since consumers are willing to pay in order that the season may be prolonged, Italy and France are able to take advantage of their climate to send in early supplies. With an article which is regarded as necessary all the year and is also readily transported, such as onions, imports may be obtained from very distant sources.

It may be argued that an important factor in the situation which has been described is the structure of tariffs. This may be discounted for two reasons. The tariff on most items was raised in 1953 and within three years the National Farmers' Union applied for further increases in order to safeguard British producers. These additional tariff increases were not granted though some tariffs have been raised since 1953. In 1960 and subsequently, legislation has been passed providing grants, subsidies, etc., aimed at the long-term improvement in efficiency in the horticulture industry that will make protection no longer necessary. On the other hand, the level of tariffs varies according to the season and is generally adjusted to give maximum protection at those times of the year when the local supply is inadequate and imports are available more cheaply. Thus the seasonal pattern of imports arises despite and not because of the level of protection offered to home producers. Indeed, the structure of tariffs provides additional evidence for the reality of the spatial changes in supplies from one month to the next.

It may be objected that dairy products and horticultural crops represent special cases and that conclusions based on the study of them do not have general application. But the imports of such commodities constitute 10 per cent of total United Kingdom imports and 25 per cent of all imports of food, beverages and tobacco. Over a quarter of gross agricultural income in the United Kingdom is derived from milk and milk products, and nearly a tenth from horticultural products.[28] Granting that these items are not typical of agricultural production in general—which is too diverse for any product or group of products to be typical—nevertheless they represent a very important sector of the agricultural economy. Furthermore, these are among the products which, with rising standards of living, are becoming increasingly significant in relation to other types of food, at any rate in the more developed countries.

More important, we can see elements of the same pattern in the other sectors of British agriculture and imports. Fat-stock contribute more to the gross income earned by British farmers than any other type of enterprise, just over 30 per cent. Home production accounts for 97 per cent of pork supplies, 41 per cent of mutton and lamb and 74 per cent of beef and veal. The relatively large import of mutton and lamb in comparison with beef imports is related to two considerations. It appears that beef is subject to greater deterioration as a result of refrigeration (consequent upon freezing and thawing) than is the case with mutton and lamb, with the result that imported beef is a relatively inferior meat and tends to command a proportionately lower price. Second, wool is produced jointly with mutton and lamb; hides jointly with beef. Wool commands a very high price in relation to its bulk, much higher than the price fetched by hides. The joint product mutton-wool incurs a proportionately smaller transport cost in relation to value than does the product beef-hides and this is an important consideration in explaining the greater proportion of mutton which is imported.

The large quantity of pork which is home-produced appears to be due to several factors operating together. There are stringent health regulations to prevent the disease trichinosis entering the country; this parasite is carried in pig flesh and can only be destroyed by cooking or curing the meat. The disease is common in some continental countries, though it is not found in other countries, such as New Zealand. Second, pork tends to deteriorate substantially at the time of freezing (or chilling) and thawing, more so than other meats on account of the content and nature of the fat. This means that the export of fresh pork is relatively less worth while than the export of mutton and beef, or of cured pig meat: the point is confirmed by the fact that much of the fresh pork which is imported is used for curing. Third, the market for pork in this country is curiously irregular, not only from season to season but also from year to year, and this seriously inhibits specialist production for export.

To complete the discussion of British agriculture, a few words must be said about grain production. One of the important things to notice is that the yields of grain crops in this country, in common with north-west Europe, are much higher than in the countries which provide the main export supplies. This is readily apparent from Table 13. Two reasons may be adduced. The first is that climatic and soil conditions in Britain and Europe are more suitable for heavy yields than are those found in Argentina, Australia and elsewhere. Second, that in this island and neighbouring countries there is a multitude of products which may profitably by produced, whereas in the arid plains which are far removed from markets the alternatives are minimal. If grains are going to be produced at all in this country, intensive production is imperative because other crops are readily available and eagerly compete for the farmers' attention.

TABLE 13

WHEAT YIELD, METRIC TONS PER HECTARE,
1948–9 TO 1952–3 AND 1962–3 TO 1964–5

	1948–9 to 1952–3	*1962–3 to 1964–5*		*1948–9 to 1952–3*	*1962–3 to 1964–5*
Denmark	3·65	4·03	Canada	1·28	1·51
Netherlands	3·64	4·49	Argentina	1·15	1·66
Belgium	3·22	3·97	Australia	1·12	1·32
United Kingdom	2·72	4·13	United States	1·12	1·72

Source: F.A.O., *Production Yearbook, 1965*, 1966, pp. 39–40.

A further important feature is the use to which the grain is put. In Britain, during the period 1962–3 to 1964–5, concentrates—which virtually are grains—retained on the farm of origin averaged 3·5 million metric tons annually, representing 28 per cent of all grain output. A further 5·6 million tons (44 per cent of output) were sold as stockfeed for use on other farms.[29] Thus, 72 per cent of all grain output was directed toward animal husbandry and this proportion was much higher than in the period 1954–5 to 1956–7, when it was 57 per cent. Clearly, grain production is an integral part of the meat and dairy enterprises and consequently reflects the consideration of proximity to markets, even though indirectly.

With other products, as with grains, it is important to notice that the guaranteed prices, subsidies, import duties and quotas affect the level of production rather than the nature of products obtained from our farms. It cannot be said that such measures are the fundamental cause for the main character of British farming, only that they influence the general level of output and have some impact on the proportions of product.

Other cases

Let us turn very briefly to an examination of some findings relating to countries other than the United Kingdom. In the succeeding paragraphs, only a selection of examples is offered, sufficient to establish the generality of what has been said already. The reader will be aware of additional examples which have not been quoted; to include all the available examples would in itself require a whole book. At a relatively small scale, two recent studies attract our attention. In a doctoral dissertation, Stamer[30] analysed the distribution of agriculture around the city of Hamburg, which forms the main centre of consumption of local produce. Using 1950 production and crop area data by the smallest German administrative unit, the *Gemeinde*, and plotting distributions by units of 10 hectares, he showed that an irregular concentric zoning of land uses obtains. The fundamental factor causing this he found to be distance from Hamburg, with modifications to the ideal pattern arising from conditions of the physical environment. His findings are summarized below:

Zone 1	City	
	Allotments	
Zone 2	Commercial horticulture	Irregular distribution in this inner zone on
	Fruit	account of differing soil conditions.
	Osiers	
	Nurseries	
Zone 3	Arable farming	Cattle to the west—lowland.
	Cattle farming	Arable to the east—better drained land.

Phlipponneau[31] has traced the evolution of land-use patterns in the environs of Paris from the end of the fourteenth century to the present day. One of the striking things which emerges is the persistence with which enterprises such as fruit and vegetable production, cut flowers and nurseries cling to the skirts of the French capital. The less intensive forms of agriculture, arable farming and stock raising, are forced to occupy the territory further away.

At the European scale, one of the most thorough studies of agricultural regions is that published by Jonasson, which, despite subsequent agricultural changes, is still broadly correct. After an exposition of some of von Thünen's ideas, he characterized western Europe in the following terms:

Northwest Europe may be regarded as one vast conurbation, and considered as one geographic center of consumption and market facilities for the agricultural products of the entire inner belt of horticulture, olericulture, dairying and other intensive land uses. . . .[32]

The point is confirmed by a map which van Valkenburg and Held have prepared[33] showing that the average yield of eight crops declines with increasing distance from the area of most intensive farming centred on the Low Countries, Denmark and south-east England (see Fig. 7). The regularity of the decline in yields is astonishing. In a recent study of the agriculture of Natal, Hurwitz came to the conclusion that

A striking feature of this study has been the development of the major production zones in conformity with land-use theory. Land use can be explained by the principle of comparative advantage. . . .[34]

He enumerated physical and social factors, but laid stress on von Thünen's ideas as the dominant consideration, zones of land use centring on Durban and cutting across physical boundaries. Another example comes from west Africa: Kayser and Tricart prepared maps of the production of groundnuts in Senegal for three separate years —1900, 1937 and 1950—identifying areas of considerable, medium and slight production. Groundnuts are a cash crop, the greater part of production being exported. In each year, the zone of most intensive production lay near the coast, the area of sparse output inland, where transport was more difficult and costly. Whereas in 1900 cultivation ceased at about 200 kilometres from Dakar, by 1950 the limit was 600 kilometres and the area of considerable yield had extended over regions of moderate output, which in turn had encroached on localities where formerly production was scanty or non-existent.[35] Throughout West Africa, the major cities have their own zones for the supply of staple foodstuffs which rarely extend to more than 80 or 160 kilometres[36] and even in the case of Tokyo the greater part of fresh vegetables is supplied from within 42 kilometres of the centre of the metropolis.[37]

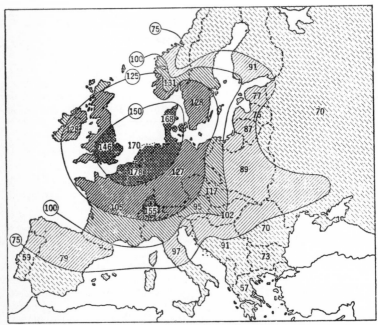

Fig. 7   Intensity of agriculture in Europe. The index of 100 is the average European yield per acre of eight main crops: wheat, rye, barley, oats, corn, potatoes, sugar beet and hay. 1937 political boundaries. (Reproduced from *Europe* by S. van Valkenburg and C. C. Held, second edn., 1952, by permission of John Wiley and Sons, Inc.)

The world pattern of trade in wheat was analysed by Lösch[38] for the harvest year 1928–9, the last year before considerable government intervention upset the 'normal' situation. He found that when the confusing medley of trade statistics was examined carefully, each exporting country had a distinct marketing zone closely related to the ease of transport. These zones expanded and contracted according to the season but constituted essentially rational arrangements when it is remembered that there are different types of wheat suitable for different purposes.

In his classic study, *Interregional and International Trade*, Ohlin categorically averred that 'international trade theory cannot be understood except in relation to and as a part of general localization theory . . .'[39] He devoted several chapters to the problems and effects of the cost of moving goods, showing how the patterns of trade between areas are intimately affected by the costs of transport. Though his centre of interest was trade as such, he showed that to consider trading relationships a close understanding of the conditions influencing production and its location is an essential part of the analysis.

Examples of the influence of distance are easy to find, although affected by many varying circumstances at the same time. If Denmark exports butter and eggs to Great Britain, while Australia sends wool, the explanation is partly to be found in the different distances to market. (Ohlin, p. 148.)

The particular lead given by Ohlin, who derived inspiration from Weber, has been followed more by persons interested in location than by workers in the field of trade: Lösch and Isard come to mind as the more important followers. However, there have been some attempts to measure the influence of distance upon trading relationships, of which we may note Beckerman's[40] finding that the amount of commerce transacted between the European nations in the years 1938, 1948 and 1953 was measurably affected by the distance separating them. The correlations he obtained are mostly significant and prove, if proof be needed, the importance of transport costs in influencing the quantity and nature of trade.

At this point, we are brought into the middle of a whole field of literature concerned with the influence which one phenomenon has upon another according to the distance separating them. The basic analogy is with a gravitational field where one heavenly body exerts a pull on all others—a pull which varies according to the size or mass of the bodies concerned and inversely with the square of the intervening distance. Much of the pioneer work along these lines was done by sociologists and marketing experts, interested in personal and economic interactions as affected by distance, but the concept has been applied and elaborated by economists and geo-

D

graphers.[41] Though one may quarrel with some of the applications, it is important to recognize that the present study links up with these others in the similarity of underlying concept.

By way of addendum, it were as well to recall that although this chapter has been framed very largely in terms of marketing produce, nevertheless the question of inputs required for farming does arise at the regional and world scales, even in the present day. Tractors are more costly to buy and maintain in the remoter parts of Brazil and India than in the United States and western Europe. Within a country, there may be spatial variations in some prices, as is the case with petrol in Uganda; in the remoter regions, it is 15 per cent dearer than in the vicinity of Kampala, whence supplies are shipped.[42] A point of considerable future interest is the development of mechanized composting techniques and improved methods of treating sewerage to obtain the sludge as fertilizer. It is where urban populations are large that such practices are being adopted as a means of preventing river pollution and to reduce the cost of carting and tipping refuse. We are returning to the situation in which the major centres of population are sources of manure, either animal or human, and the Asiatic countries may be able to pass straight from the era of 'night soil' to the era of municipally vended compost and sludge. We may expect to notice agricultural changes in response to the availability of these manures in the vicinity of the conurbations and large cities.[43]

BIBLIOGRAPHICAL NOTES

1. W. H. Smith, 'Refrigeration and the marketing of watercress', *Agriculture*, 1958, pp. 132–5.

2. See for example: S. Daggett, *Principles of Inland Transportation*, 1955; M. R. Bonavia, *The Economics of Transport*, 1955: D. P. Locklin, *The Economics of Transportation*, 3rd edn., 1947.

3. W. A. Mackintosh, *Prairie Settlement: the Geographical Setting*, 1934. See also: A. Fishlow, *American Railroads and the Transformation of the Ante-Bellum Economy*, 1965.

4. E. Dunsdorfs, *The Australian Wheat-Growing Industry, 1788–1948*, 1956, pp. 163–4.

5. R. G. Albion, *Forests and Sea Power: the Timber Problem of the Royal Navy, 1652–1862*, 1926, p. 102.

6. T. S. Willan, *River Navigation in England, 1600–1750*, 1936.

7. A recent work which summarizes much of the available literature (mostly American) is *Highway Development and Geographic Change*, W. L. Garrison *et al.*, 1959.

8. H. Nicolaï and J. Jacques, 'La transformation des paysages congolais par le chemin de fer. L'example du B.C.K.', *Mémoires*, Institut Royal Colonial Belge, Section des Sciences Naturelles et Médicales, 1954, pp. 7–208.

9. Nicolaï and Jacques, 1954, *supra*, p. 47.

10. J. E. Parsons, 'Bananas in Ecuador: a new chapter in the history of tropical agriculture,' *Economic Geography*, 1957, p. 204. The position is confirmed by D. A. Preston, 'Changes in the economic geography of banana production in Ecuador', *Transactions*, Institute of British Geographers, no. 37, 1965, p. 79.

11. J. B. Wills (Ed.), *Agriculture and Land Use in Ghana*, 1962, p. 177.

12. *The Times*, 13 November 1959.

13. P. Monbeig, *Pionniers et Planteurs de São Paulo*, 1952, p. 204.

14. Royal Commission, 1955, *supra* (ch. 4), p. 120.

15. F. J. Fisher, 'The development of the London food market, 1540–1640', *Economic History Review*, 1934–5, no. 2, pp. 46–64. For a summary account that incorporates other material, see: J. Thirsk (Ed.), *The Agrarian History of England and Wales, Vol. IV, 1500–1640*, 1967, pp. 507–16.

16. N. S. B. Gras, *The Evolution of the English Corn Market*, 1915, p. 122.

17. D. Defoe, *A Tour Through England and Wales*, Everyman, 1948.

18. E. W. Gilboy, *Wages in Eighteenth Century England*, 1934, p. 39, quoting Arthur Young.

19. G. B. G. Bull, 'Thomas Milne's land utilization map of the London Area in 1800', *Geographical Journal*, 1956, p. 28; W. G. East, 'Land utilization in England at the end of the eighteenth century', *Geographical Journal*, 1937, pp. 156–72.

20. H. and J. von Oppenfield, J. C. St Iglesia and P. R. Sandoval, *Farm Management, Land Use and Tenancy in the Philippines*, Central Experiment Station, Bulletin no. 1, 1957, p. 132.

21. Departmental Committee on Distribution and Prices of Agricultural Produce (Linlithgow Report), *Interim Report on Milk and Milk Products*, 1924; F. J. Prewett, *The Marketing of Farm Produce: Part II, Milk*, 1927; E. H. Whetham, 'The London milk trade, 1860–1900', *Economic History Review*, 1964, pp. 369–80.

22. F. A. Barnes, 'Dairying in Angelsey', *Transactions and Papers*, Institute of British Geographers, 1955, pp. 137–55.

23. E. Strauss and E. H. Churcher, 'The regional analysis of the milk market', *Journal of Agricultural Economics*, 1967, pp. 221–36.

24. Ministry of Agriculture, Fisheries and Food, *Horticulture in Britain. Pt. I, Vegetables*, 1967, p. 44.

25. S. Florence, 'The Selection of Industries Suitable for Dispersion into Rural Areas', *Journal*, Royal Statistical Society, 1944, pp. 93–107.

26. Ministry of Agriculture, Fisheries and Foods, 1967, *supra*, p. 45. See also: R. H. Best and R. M. Gasson, 'The changing location of intensive crops', *Studies in Rural Land Use*, Wye College, 1966.

27. *The Times*, 22 June 1966.

28. K. E. Hunt and K. R. Clark, *The State of British Agriculture 1965–6*, 1966, p. 86.

29. Idem, pp. 69 and 103.

30. H. H. Stamer, *Die Standortsorientierung der Landwirtschaft um den Gross-markt Hamburg*, dissertation, Kiel, 1952.

31. M. Phlipponneau, *La Vie Rurale de la Banlieue Parisienne*, 1956.

32. O. Jonasson, 1925, *supra* (ch. 2), pp. 289–90.

33. S. van Valkenburg and C. C. Held, *Europe*, 2nd edn., 1952, p. 102.

34. N. Hurwitz, *Agriculture in Natal 1860–1950*, 1957, p. 106.

35. B. Kayser and J. Tricart, 'Rail et route au Sénégal', *Annales de Géographie*, 1957, pp. 328–50.

36. B. F. Johnson, *The Staple Food Economies of Western Tropical Africa*, 1958, p. 15.

37. J. D. Eyre, 'Sources of Tokyo's fresh food supply', *Geographical Review*, 1959, p. 458.

38. Lösch, 1954, *supra* (ch. 1), pp. 420–7.

39. B. Ohlin, *Interregional and International Trade*, 1933, p. 142.

40. W. Beckerman, 'Distance and the pattern of intra-European trade', *Review of Economics and Statistics*, 1956, pp. 31–40.

41. G. K. Zipf, *Human Behaviour and the Principle of Least Effort*, 1949. For a brief survey of some of the literature and certain recent developments, see W. Warntz, *Toward a Geography of Price*, 1959, and Isard, 1956, *supra* (ch. 1).

42. A. M. O'Connor, *Railways and Development in Uganda*, 1965, p. 31.

43. *The Times*, 13 July 1959.

6

THE ANALYSIS INVERTED

The examination in the last two chapters of the land-use patterns which develop round settlements has been based on the assumption that the location of the settlement or major concentration of population is given and fixed. But is not much of the zoning of types and intensities of land uses, which we have ascribed to distance, in reality due to conditions of the physical environment? For example, is it not the case that often the poorer soils are reserved for grazing, these soils being situated away from the village, while the better soils which are more suited to arable cultivation are found nearer at hand? Or that the interior of Australia is much drier and more impoverished than the littoral regions where the main population centres are found, which means there is inevitably a systematic arrangement of land uses so that the intensity of use falls as one moves further away from the main markets? There is indeed much truth in this objection. At first sight, this admission may seem to limit the validity of the case to those circumstances in which the physical conditions of climate, soil, relief, etc., are approximately uniform over the area in question. But this is not so. If we cease to assume that the location of settlements is predetermined, then the principles which have been described can be inverted: if natural conditions and therefore land uses are taken as given, then the location of the settlements may be regarded as variable.

This chapter seeks to elaborate this other aspect of location analysis to prepare the way for Chapter 7 and Chapter 8. To simplify exposition, the argument is related to the location of villages and farmsteads, which has the additional advantage of introducing the next chapter; but the principle is of general application, as will be shown in Chapter 8.

Relations of a village to the resources exploited

To begin with a simplified example, we may imagine the establishment of a new agricultural settlement in an area of country not previously inhabited. Such a settlement has two sets of space-relationships of the utmost importance: one is the relationship to its lands and the other is its links with the outside world—lines of communication and other inhabited centres. It will be convenient to treat these two sets of considerations separately, dealing first with the relationship of the settlement to the resources of its territory.

Let us imagine a people of modest cultural achievements, such as the Anglo-Saxon colonists who settled widely over England. Such people, in seeking places in which to build their abodes, would have had to bear in mind the availability of arable and grazing lands, the supply of water for man and beast, fuel resources and the ease of obtaining building materials. In addition, there would be special local considerations, such as defence, the need to avoid lands liable to flooding and the ravages of malaria. But for the moment these latter may be ignored, attention being concentrated upon the universal economic needs of an agricultural community.

Fig. 8 shows the five basic elements of such a settler community's economy: with none can the settlement dispense. As we have already seen, the disadvantages posed by distance in conducting various enterprises are very variable and in the figure some hypothetical values have been assigned for each element showing the relative disadvantage of distance. These may be thought of as units of cost to the community; for example, the removal of water 1 kilometre is equivalent to 10 units of cost, whereas if the source of building materials is that far away it represents only one-tenth of the cost. It is not particularly important to discuss what the precise relative costs are, if only because they are in fact very variable both in space and time. Water has been given a high value on account of its traditional importance: it has to be used at frequent intervals in the day and is difficult to carry and store in large quantities when only elementary implements are available, such as pitchers and gourds. Arable land is usually more greedy of labour than grassland, requiring more cultivation and more transport of goods to and fro, while in the traditional rural economy over much of Europe, grazing and fuel were closely associated, both being found on the commons. Finally, building materials have been given the least weight because though they are bulky and awkward to handle they are required only at spasmodic intervals.

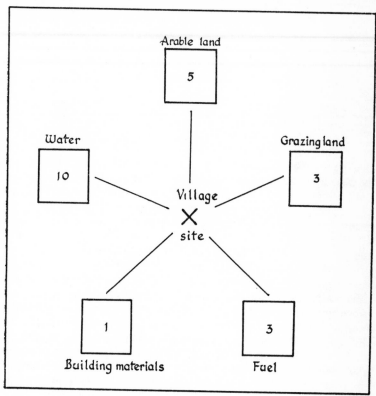

Fig. 8   Village location

The manner in which these relationships operate can best be described by considering two hypothetical village locations, x and y, which are alternatives the one to the other. A survey of the two situations might show that the various resources were situated at the distances indicated in Table 14 from the spot where the village would be built. Column D shows the cost of exploiting a particular kind of resource at the given distance of so many kilometres from the proposed village site. Location y has the smallest sum of such costs,

TABLE 14

TWO HYPOTHETICAL VILLAGE LOCATIONS

A	B Distance from village in kms.		C Units of cost per km. from village	D Product of B × C	
Resource	x	y		x	y
Water	0·1	0·5	10	1·0	5·0
Arable land	2·0	1·0	5	10·0	5·0
Grazing land	2·5	1·5	3	7·5	4·5
Fuel	2·5	2·0	3	7·5	6·0
Building materials	3·0	2·0	1	3·0	2·0
				29·0	22·5

despite the fact of being well removed from water, and there would be a clear advantage in choosing it in preference to x.

Expressed in these terms, the analysis is identical in principle to that developed by Weber, with one reservation. He was considering manufacturing industry supplied with mineral raw materials and sending the products to urban markets. The mines, the factory and the markets could all be regarded as infinitely small points of no areal extent. Such a concept clearly does not apply in the above case, since all the resources, with the possible exception of water, are distributed widely, and only the village itself approximates to a dimensionless point. This problem may be resolved in the following fashion: consider, for example, the arable land, which may be divided into numerous plots or may in imagination be carved up into units of one hectare apiece. In considering each segment, no great error is made if we assume that all the work and produce of the segment pertains to a single point located at the centre. Thus, the total 'weight' for the arable land may be obtained as the sum of the 'weights' which properly belong to each unit area. The same device may equally well be applied to the other resources which have a wide spatial extent, and so the problem of locating a settlement with respect to the lands which are to be exploited by it can be tackled in the Weberian manner.

The process of choosing a situation in which to establish one or more habitations is an exercise in least-cost location analysis, if the economic aims of the community are assumed to be given. So far as the productive objectives of the community are not immutably fixed, it is an exercise in maximum profit location, for energies released by the choice of an optimum location may be put to additional productive uses.

Yet it is one thing to recognize the constraining influence of physical obstacles which cannot readily be surmounted in an age of simple techniques and quite another to suppose that the shape of the settlements was always appropriate to the nature of the terrain. A geographical fatalism which rests upon the assumption that imperfect skill is consistently applied with perfect intelligence stands self-condemned. Ignorance, prejudice, 'historical' factors connected with the local circumstances of land-ownership, accidents of various kinds, and mere inertia, must all be allowed a part in determining both the form of the settlement and the direction of economic activity in individual cases.[1]

With these words, Lennard admonishes us not to imagine that one set of considerations has overriding priority in all circumstances; he thereby admits its importance. The significance of the location problem has been even more explicitly noticed by Orwin:

A study of the map in any region of hill and valley shows how parish boundaries were defined by farming considerations. Taking extreme examples so as to demonstrate the point more clearly, it may be shown how the need for shelter, for water, for grazing-land and land for tillage, in the proportions necessary to sustain the community, determined the size and shape of the allocation of land which came, ultimately, to form the parish.[2]

Orwin then proceeds to examine two areas in detail, parts of Berkshire and Lincolnshire, showing how the elongation of the parishes in relation to the siting of the villages along the scarp foot enabled each community economically to command the full range of local resources, the wet grasslands of the lowland, the light ploughland at the scarp foot and the downland grazing above. These are particularly obvious cases, but the principle has wide application:

The principles which actuated these early [Saxon] cultivators in the organization of their townships and farms were economic and technical, and they were everywhere observed, in all the farming districts of England, even though often less obviously.[3]

The same point has been made by East with respect to settlements in Europe:

The several types of land, distinguished on the ground of their usefulness to man, were ... attached to a village and organised for exploitation according to certain systems and to customary practices, [and] were combined together in a certain proportion, so as best to satisfy human needs.[4]

A point to observe in relation to the above is the important rôle of water. It is commonly noticed how settlements in Europe are generally very closely related to water sources and so it is often inferred that this 'determines' the location of villages. It should be evident, however, that water merely has a great importance relative to other requirements, which is a sufficient reason for locating near the source of supply. In the case of the scarp-foot villages found in England, such a location also happens to be the one which minimizes the costs of conducting the various enterprises found in the traditional village economy.

Under other circumstances, location with respect to water may not be so important. For the Ngwa of south-east Nigeria, 'convenience with regard to agricultural land and not the location of water is the most important factor in determining the settlement site',[5] and the distance from permanent water may be as much as 13 kilometres. In Eastern Nigeria as a whole, about half the rural population lives more than 5 kilometres from perennial streams.[6] Although the women and children may spend four or five hours daily in furnishing water for the household, this is mainly a dry-season task when there is comparatively little else to do, since nearby ponds supply most needs during the wet season.

If the historical evidence is amenable only to inference and not proof, then the importance of lands in the location of the settlement is confirmed by the behaviour of shifting cultivators. Before they were resettled in permanent abodes, the Azande always chose a very fertile strip of the soil catena, immediately above the gallery forest which marches along the valley floor. Here they found a rich sandy loam covered with a transition forest which could easily be cleared and where they could create their intensively cultivated gardens. Further afield, on the poorer sections of the catena, temporary clearances would be made for the much more extensive cultivation of millet and other crops. This position had the further advantage of providing easy access to the stream below for water. Such a location was invariably chosen in preference to any other point on the catena, even though the choice was overtly made on oracular authority. The wisdom of the oracle lay in its recognition of sound economic principles, choosing sites which minimized the efforts involved in winning a livelihood.[7] Other shifting cultivators display a similar skill in choosing the site of a new abode, as in north-west Rhodesia.[8]

The argument of the preceding paragraphs is not impaired when we introduce considerations such as defence, the avoidance of malarial areas and avalanches. These additional requirements of a settlement site merely reduce the number of choices which are open and make the balancing of economic and non-economic advantages and disadvantages necessary. If defence is an important need, then the advantages of hill-top positions are signalled, whether Uffington Castle on Whitehorse Hill or the seven hills of Rome. But it is not any hill that will be selected—only a hill which, while meeting defence requirements, also permits the community to conduct its normal business without undue inconvenience. In practice, the best local defensive site may make life impossibly difficult owing to the separation of dwelling and cultivated land which its occupation would require, and some compromise will be adopted which reduces the military advantage somewhat but increases the economic benefit, the balance struck depending on the circumstances of time and place. Exactly the same argument applies in respect of the other additional considerations.

So far we have dealt with villages in particular, but identical considerations apply at the scale of the individual farm, using the same formulation. As with the village, the greatest weight generally attaches to the supply of water, followed by that land which is the most intensively cultivable; the terrain suitable for less intensive use can most conveniently be the furthest removed.

External relations of a settlement

But it is not sufficient to consider merely the relationship of a settlement to its lands, since only an entirely self-sufficient community has no need of regular friendly external contacts. Such communities probably no longer exist and in any case have never been particularly important except in very remote times. Most peoples have friendly contacts of one kind or another with their neighbours and facilitating such intercourse is a cogent consideration in the choice of a location; certainly, it has become increasingly important with the passage of time, as the degree of local self-sufficiency has declined. Traditionally, the main link with other communities was through the travelling of persons and the interchange of goods, which render location on or near lines of communication an advantage. The more important these external transactions are, the greater significance attaches to access to land, river or sea routes, and the greater the advantage of a location with good external communications. The choice of a situation for a settlement would therefore depend upon a balance of considerations: the ease of conducting the internal economy of the community and the ease of concluding the external transactions. In this sense, such locations may still be viewed in terms of the Weberian system, for Weber considered both the assembly of raw materials for manufacture and the distribution of the goods to the respective markets, a least-cost location being obtained in respect of each part and the over-all least-cost situation being derived from the combination of both. In the case we are considering, sales of produce and services elsewhere are equivalent to the distribution of goods to the market; the purchase of goods and services from outside is analogous to the assembly of raw materials at the point of production.

The principle can be applied fairly easily to settlements that are part of a hierarchical system, as is normally the case in Europe and as is envisaged in most theoretical studies of settlement organization (e.g., Christaller and Lösch). In a hierarchical system, trade transactions take place in a well-defined manner between settlements of higher and lower order, so that the direction and nature of the trade links can be established with some degree of precision. In other contexts, however, trade takes place on a large scale between settlements of the same order and it may be very difficult to identify the pattern relevant for any one settlement. This is especially the case among the Yoruba-speaking people of Western Nigeria, whose settlements are organized in market circuits of varying periodicity (four days, eight days, etc.). Each day, a market is held but at a different site. Hence, the relevant unit to consider may not be a single village or town but a group of settlements that is organized over a sizeable territory.[9]

Consideration must also be given to other external links in the form of electricity supplies, water and sewerage facilities, telephone and postal services. Most of what needs to be said on this subject is most conveniently reserved to subsequent chapters: in Chapter 7, the importance of such considerations in laying out new settlements in reclamation areas is treated; while the significance of these technical developments for already established populations is tackled in Chapter 9. One general point may be made at this juncture: in the provision of all these services, considerable economies are obtained when the population is concentrated. The more scattered the populace the more costly is the provision of these amenities. Consequently the more remote spots are the last to receive these modern benefits; and as these external links become more important, the advantages of concentrating a dispersed population are becoming greater than formerly was the case.

There is very little quantitative evidence to show the magnitude of the savings which accrue from bringing together scattered dwellings. In any case, the pricing policies adopted by electricity or water authorities, for example, are often such that the individual consumer does not bear the full cost of provision, which makes the task of analysing the matter even more difficult. However, one example can be given which illustrates the point very aptly. From a study of the cost of collecting milk from farms in England and Wales and taking it to the local depot for bulking for onward consignment, it was found that the collection cost varied very closely with the number of gallons collected per mile travelled by the lorry.

TABLE 15[10]

ENGLAND AND WALES, 1956: COMPUTED COSTS OF
MILK COLLECTION FOR CONTRACTORS HANDLING
OVER TWO MILLION GALLONS ANNUALLY

Gallons of milk per vehicle mile	Pence per gallon
5	3·786
10	1·678
20	0·883
40	0·582

Gallons per vehicle mile is a measure of the degree of local concentration or dispersal of milk production for sale, compounded of the number of farms, the production of milk per farm and the arrangement of the public highway in relation to the farmsteads. From the one point of view of off-farm collection costs, a high degree of local concentration of milk production is evidently highly desirable. In this particular case, it is the Milk Marketing Board that incurs the additional cost of collection in areas of sparse milk sales and reaps the benefit of economies where much is collected locally, as the price received by the farmer does not reflect at all fully the differences in collection costs. Thus, if there is any incentive towards the local concentration of milk production to maximize the number of gallons collected per vehicle mile, it is felt more by the Board than by the farmers.

The same principle—that concentration confers economies of provision—applies to other services, but it is not possible to assess the magnitudes involved, and it should not be inferred that the case of milk collection is representative.

The next chapter takes up and elaborates at the small scale the theme which has been developed in this chapter, and the subsequent one turns attention to the larger scale of phenomena.

BIBLIOGRAPHICAL NOTES

1. R. Lennard, *Rural England, 1086–1135: a Study of Social and Agrarian Conditions*, 1959, p. 269.

2. C. S. Orwin and C. S. Orwin, *The Open Fields*, 2nd edn., 1954, p. 24.

3. *Idem*, p. 27.

4. W. G. East, *An Historical Geography of Europe*, 4th edn., 1956, p. 98.

5. W. B. Morgan, 'Farming practice, settlement pattern and population density in south-eastern Nigeria', *Geographical Journal*, 1955, p. 321.

6. Y. Karmon, 'A geography of settlement in Eastern Nigeria', *Studies in Geography*, The Hebrew University, Jerusalem, 1966, p. 47.

7. de Schlippé, 1956, *supra* (ch. 4).

8. C. G. Trapnell and J. N. Clothier, *The Soils, Vegetation and Agricultural Systems of North Western Rhodesia*, 1936, especially pp. 23–57.

9. B. W. Hodder, 'Distribution of markets in Yorubaland', *Scottish Geographical Magazine*, 1965, pp. 48–58.

10. M. Chisholm, 'Regional variations in road transport costs: milk collection from farms in England and Wales', *Farm Economist*, 1957, p. 36.

7

THE FARMSTEAD AND THE VILLAGE

Some of the further applications of the principles of location as they operate at the small scale of the individual farmstead or village are now examined. The present purpose is to discuss a number of issues in which the problems posed by distance form an important or dominant theme, albeit only one of several significant considerations. The arrangement of the material of this chapter presented considerable problems, for a seemingly motley collection of topics is relevant, drawn from the present and the past and taken from various parts of the world, though most of the examples are from Europe. The most satisfactory arrangement seemed to be to take the material in its generic relationships, at the expense of continuity in space and time. Thus, after a summary statement of the costs of cultivation related to different patterns of settlement, the question of dispersal of dwellings from previously compact settlements is discussed, followed by an analysis of certain problems related to dispersed settlement based largely on experience with new colonization of reclaimed land. Then come some comments on the difficulties encountered in pursuing the reverse policy, of concentrating a previously dispersed rural population into villages, and after that a discussion of the common habit of maintaining satellite settlements and a related process of colonization. Finally, the significance of location in administering land taxes and for the application of work-study techniques is dealt with.

To recapitulate our earlier findings, Table 16 has been prepared, based on an estimate of the extent to which the net return per hectare declines with distance, an extent which is intermediate between the precipitate diminution found to prevail in Finland and the lesser rate of decline indicated for the Netherlands and Pakistan (Chapter 4):

TABLE 16

ESTIMATED EFFECT OF DISTANCE BETWEEN SETTLEMENTS UPON
THE AVERAGE NET PRODUCT PER HECTARE

Distance between settlements in kms.	Average distance to cultivated land in kms.	Average net product per hectare, zero distance to land equals 100
0·5	0·18	94
1·0	0·35	90
1·5	0·53	85
2·0	0·70	80
3·0	1·10	72
4·0	1·40	66
6·0	2·11	55
8·0	2·81	47

It has been assumed that all the rural populace lives in nucleated villages of no spatial extent which are distributed regularly, each surrounded by its own territory in the form of a regular hexagon. Since each settlement does in fact have a finite area, the average distance from the farmsteads to the attached land may be slightly less than from the centre of the village, while a further factor contributing to an over-statement of the loss associated with distance is the omission of any consideration of dispersed settlement around the villages. This bias is compensated for by the fact that the territory associated with a village is usually very variable in shape, with the consequence that, for a given average distance between settlements or given area of territory, the average distance to the land is greater than for a regular hexagon.[1]

Thus, the figures in Table 16 should be taken only as representing a rough order of magnitude. In the construction of this table, the distance between settlements was taken as the datum from which to calculate distances to the land. For practical purposes in relation to particular cases, it would be more satisfactory to start from figures for the actual distances separating fields and dwellings; but, as far as I am aware, there are only two readily available sets of data which give regional differences of distance, and since these give only averages and no information on the dispersions, no very satisfactory estimate of regional differences in cultivation costs can be made from them. However, the cadastral and/or tax records of many countries must contain the necessary data, though often they are not readily accessible. Given the requisite figures, a very fruitful method of classifying settlement patterns could be based upon the distance between farmstead and field, which would provide material invaluable for planning and development and significant in describing the relationships between man and his physical environment, probably more useful than is vouchsafed by the currently popular methods of measuring the degree of dispersal and nucleation.

Dispersal of settlements

In an attempt to improve the rural standard of living in southern Italy, Sicily and Sardinia, the Italian government is carrying out an extensive programme of rural transformation. The works being conducted there are resulting in a considerable re-location of farmsteads, one important object being to reduce the losses arising from the excessive distances which sunder home and work. This re-location of the peasantry upon the holdings they themselves operate has been made possible by three developments of the utmost importance. First, as elsewhere in the world, pacification and the establishment of law and order make it unnecessary to concentrate the population into easily defended settlements able to ward off the marauders who were wont to rob and pillage. Second, technical developments in the manufacture of aqueducts and conduits, pipes and pumps, have greatly enhanced the facility with which water may be transported over considerable distances and distributed to individually small consumers. Water for human and animal use may be had at an almost infinitely large number of points, instead of being confined to a limited number of stream, lake or well sites; and irrigation has also been made easier. Third, the use of D.D.T. and other measures of control has banished from many areas the scourge of malaria, thus making habitable territory which formerly was shunned.

The surplus of labour in agriculture—estimated to have been somewhat under 20 per cent of the working population unemployed or under-employed—considered with the inability of industry to absorb sufficient new workers, restricted emigration opportunities and limited resources of unused land, bespoke the necessity for intensifying agricultural production to raise living standards. With this object in view, the Italian government instituted in 1950 a series of measures of land reform and agricultural improvement: extensive areas have been irrigated or transformed by the introduction of tree crops, such as olives, almonds, figs and vines, and by more intensive methods of cultivating grain crops. The rearing of cattle is also being encouraged. Such crops and methods are considerably more demanding of labour than the formerly customary cultivation of wheat and barley and grazing of sheep, as can be seen in Tables 6 and 7. The result is a manifold increase in the annual labour requirements per hectare, the more so where irrigation is practised, for attention must then be given to the holding at any time of the day or night.

The substitution of relatively intensive labour systems of agriculture for the previous extensive types would be prohibitively expensive were the peasantry to continue living in the agro-towns, far from their lands. The excessive concentration of population that existed before the post-war programme of land reform began is shown by the data in Table 17. The eight reform agencies, whose total area of responsibility comprises nearly one-third of Italy, had by the end of 1965 built 194 residential centres, 353 service centres and over 40,000 new farm dwellings.[2] The result is a remarkable transformation of the rural landscape: as one travels across the plains of Metaponto or Maremma, one can see for kilometre upon kilometre a guard of honour of small dwellings, regimented in regular rows, each standing in its own plot of land.

TABLE 17[3]

ITALY, 1936: CONCENTRATION OF THE RURAL POPULATION

Region	Land area per inhabited centre in sq. kms.	Average distance between centres in kms.	Average number of inhabitants per centre	Scattered population as % of that in centres
Apulia	53	7·3	6,700	7·2
Sicily	33	5·7	4,600	11·1
Basilicata	55	7·5	2,600	15·1
Lazio	20	4·4	2,400	25·0
Campania	11	3·3	2,400	20·6
Sardinia	50	7·1	2,000	8·7

Attempts have been made to assess the total increase in gross production resulting from the development schemes and some estimates put the ultimate increase at over 100 per cent. While it is too early to know what the final situation will be, a clear indication of the trend is given by the following figures, which relate to lands which have been expropriated in Italy:

TABLE 18[4]

ITALY, 1963: PERCENTAGE OF EXPROPRIATED LAND AREA
IN VARIOUS USES

Type of land use	Percentage distribution at the time of acquisition for reallocation	Percentage distribution in 1963
Arable	53·4	67·5
Tree crops	2·6	9·4
Pasture and uncultivated	35·4	16·0
Woods and forest	8·6	7·1
	100·0	100·0

The tendency is towards the more intensive types of crop and since these trends are either contrary to the experience of Italy as a whole or are more strongly marked, they may be attributed to the special experience of these areas, notably in relation to changes in ownership and settlement.

The Italian programme for rural improvement is spectacular and obvious, as also is the Dutch reclamation of the polders, and may easily divert attention from what is probably a much more significant process current throughout most of western Europe: namely, the consolidation of holdings and the concomitant re-location of farmsteads. Here there is no radical transformation of the system of farming in the way there is with the introduction of irrigation or other entirely new systems of cultivation; the effects are less in any one area but are spread much more widely. Consolidation means the re-allocation of holdings which are fragmented, the creation of farms which comprise only one or a very few parcels in place of the multitude of patches formerly in the possession of each peasant. At the same time, roads are re-aligned, drainage improved, water supplies made available, better systems of farming introduced and perhaps some farmsteads re-located. The magnitude of the task that has been undertaken by governments and private organizations in Europe is indicated by the following table based on figures assembled by Jacoby:[5]

TABLE 19

EUROPE: LAND CONSOLIDATION
(*Areas in Thousand Hectares*)

Country	Total agricultural area	Land consolidation		
		Carried out	In course of execution	To be executed (applied for)
Austria	4,082	314	46	1,180
Finland	2,879	2,319	300	Province of Vasa
France	34,567	2,020	862	14,000
W. Germany	14,383	4,320	800	5,738
Italy	20,905	15	—	10,000
Netherlands	2,306	92	171	1,466
Switzerland	2,172	231	30	485

The figures for the area of land consolidated, in course of execution and scheduled for the future, are not comparable between countries, since the meaning attached to the term 'consolidation' varies from nation to nation. Nor are the figures for agricultural areas strictly comparable with the consolidation data, as the former exclude forest lands, some of which are included in the consolidation schemes.

Wherever possible, the new holding is laid out to include the owner's residence: if this policy be pushed to its logical conclusion, the farms would tend to be triangular in shape, the apexes being in the village and containing the farmstead; the farms would form a star centred on the village.[6] Experience with this type of consolidation in Denmark and elsewhere has shown that it produces farms which are awkward to operate. It may well be that a considerable proportion of the farms could not be laid out so as to include the farmstead in its old location—especially where the villages are large. In the case of the land reform in Russia after the revolution of 1905–6, about nine out of ten new holdings did not include the farmstead of the operator.[7] Therefore, the common current policy is to move some of the farmsteads from the village on to their holdings, so that the pattern of settlement produced is one of a central village from which some farms are operated, surrounded by a number of isolated farmsteads. Such re-location, which is especially frequent in West Germany and Switzerland, occurs generally when there is land situated three or more kilometres from the village, but also when the distance to the further lands is less.[8]

These measures for the reconstruction of the countryside, to create a more dispersed form of settlement pattern, are conscious efforts to achieve a situation which has existed for many years in Norway, Sweden, the United Kingdom and Denmark. In Denmark, the movement to achieve this object gathered real momentum with the legislation of 1781 to consolidate land and of 1788 to emancipate the peasantry from its feudal bond to the soil. One result of the reforming zeal was the establishment of unitary holdings in place of the open-fields worked in common and the consequent appearance of isolated farmsteads set on their own land. As early as 1807, the process of transformation had been completed in many districts, while by 1835 practically the whole agricultural area had experienced this revolution.[9]

Perhaps the most famous example of all is the parliamentary enclosure of great tracts of England between about 1750 and 1850: this continued and completed a process that has been going on for centuries. By the use of parliamentary powers, coercion replaced consent and the rate of change was much accelerated. Under the traditional open-field system of cultivation in common, each peasant was allotted a certain number of strips, the locations of which were scattered. Quite apart from tenurial relations with regard to the lord of the manor and the necessity for communal regulation and co-operation for certain tasks, the scattering of the strips provided a cogent reason for living together in nucleated villages because this minimized the total distance from the dwellings to the parcels. Enclosure swept away the old system. In its stead, individual owner-ship of all land became normal, the strips were consolidated into unitary holdings and roads and ditches were re-aligned. Wherever possible, these new farms were laid out to include the pre-existing dwelling of the owner but many farms were inevitably situated at a considerable remove and were therefore separated from the farm-stead.

In such cases it was to the obvious advantage of the farmer to build himself a new farmstead in the middle of his lands.

This, indeed, is what happened in due course, but the old village was far from disintegrated by such new building unless it was already very small and decaying. Often many years elapsed before the village farmers built their new houses, however inconvenient it may have been to live in the centre of the parish and to farm on the boundaries. . . .

Yet the total number of farmsteads built out in the fields between the villages is very small. One would guess not more than half a dozen in the average parish, often fewer than that. . . .

Nevertheless a new element had been introduced into the landscape in this part of England—the isolated farmstead. Nearly all the farm-houses we see between the compact villages of the country between the Yorkshire and the Dorset coasts date from the century 1750–1850. The few that are older may well be either the result of Tudor or Stuart enclosure, or examples of monastic granges. . . . But probably four out of five of these farmsteads in the fields are the consequence of parliamentary enclosure.[10]

Associated with the enclosure movement were changes in farming practices. These changes varied from one part of the country to another. In the drier eastern counties, arable farming often remained the mainstay of the economy but in the west much arable land was laid down to pasture. Particularly during the Napoleonic wars and the immediately following decades, agricultural products were scarce and fetching high prices, which tended to encourage an intensification of farming, a process made easier by enclosure. Despite this, there are many contemporary accounts of destitution among the rural inhabitants, which has commonly been attributed to the process of enclosure itself.[11] This view has recently been challenged by Chambers,[12] who adduces evidence to show that in fact the surplus of rural population was predominantly due to a general and rapid increase of population which outstripped the capacity of the land to provide a livelihood, despite the intensification of farming. He argues that the surplus of agrarian inhabitants did not arise, as previously thought, from the dispossession of the peasants and a reduction in labour requirements arising from enclosure.

Whichever may be the true explanation, and Chambers' case has much to commend it, our location study bears on the issue in the following manner. With the reorganization of holdings and the emplacement of farmsteads on the farm territory, the amount of time lost in travelling to and fro was reduced. Studies of modern schemes of farm consolidation show that a given gross income can be produced with between 5 and 50 per cent less labour time than is needed on fragmented holdings.[13] Although some of the time saved may be put to productive uses on the farm, an increase in output can be achieved that does not require a commensurate increase in employment and may even be associated with a reduction in the labour force. Modern experience is likely to be relevant to earlier land reform programmes and therefore the factor of time saving may be regarded as accentuating the inability of agriculture to provide work for an increasing rural populace (while contributing to a higher income for those who had land or work on the land). Alternatively, if the traditional view be accepted, the element of time saving heightened the effects of the enclosure movement in creating a displaced rural 'proletariat'. Either way, the situation was made worse by the fact that many persons, especially those who formerly had rights to common grazing, now had to seek wage labour as their sole means of sustenance. Thus, the whole brunt of savings in travel time was often borne by a relatively few individuals, who became destitute, instead of being spread among the mass as an increase in leisure or in time available for productive effort. That which might have been regarded as a universal blessing if equally distributed became a calamity upon being directed at a limited number of unlucky persons.

While not wishing to exaggerate the sufferings of the rural populace or the importance of this one factor in contributing to these sufferings, it is interesting to note that exactly the same problem is being felt today, though less acutely, in parts of the world suffering from over-population and/or immobility of the rural peoples. The movement to consolidate holdings, whereby innumerable fragments of land are amalgamated into holdings comprising one block or but few, opens the way to much agricultural improvement. Commonly, this results in an increase in the level of gross and net product per hectare—intensification of farming—and a greater use of machinery, the effect of which is to curtail the labour requirements. Furthermore, the consolidation measures are usually associated with an increase in the size of holdings which causes the displacement of some farmers who cannot be found other agricultural jobs in the locality. These factors are reinforced by the savings in time which result from the consolidation schemes—savings which will be particularly great if re-location of farmsteads occurs. On the basis of assembled European evidence, Jacoby concluded that: 'With all reservations made for individual cases, it may be stated that under average conditions . . . the manpower requirements will be reduced considerably' as a result of consolidation, quoting Austrian experience that on the average the labour force is reduced by 14 per cent. One result is a diminution in the demand for hired workers; another is that a family which hires no labour may find itself possessed of more leisure time. Jacoby states that the gross yield of the holding may rise by between 20 and 70 per cent, but the full economic advantage of this increase may not be reaped unless supplementary sources of part-time employment can be provided, or full-time work outside agriculture, to enable part or all of the time saved to be put to productive purposes.

To this end, the Dutch are implementing a careful programme in an attempt to improve and rationalize the agrarian structure. Measures of consolidation are in hand which tend to reduce the need for labour and, to absorb the surplus, active steps are being taken to provide new industrial employment within the areas affected, whereby a change of work does not necessarily require a change of habitation. As a parallel measure, farms are reserved in the newly reclaimed polders to accommodate farmers displaced by the con-solidation schemes.

While the process of dispersal from existing villages is familiar to most parts of Europe at some period in history if not currently, it is not confined to this continent. Demangeon[14] described the same phenomenon in Egypt, where the establishment of scattered farm-steads has been made possible and more desirable by a technical change, the substitution of perennial irrigation for the annual in-undations of the basin system which rendered most of the territory useless for permanent homes. At the same time, improvements in the legal status of the fellaheen, whereby they may own land, with a certain loosening of the communal forms of social and economic organization, have also tended to ease dispersal, which has been quite marked since the mid-nineteenth century.

Likewise, in Thailand many small, isolated settlements and indivi-dual farmsteads have been established in the last half century. True of the central areas, this development has been especially marked in the delta region near Bangkok, throughout much of which com-pact villages have ceased to be the distinctive element of the settle-ment pattern.[15] And in Mexico, too, the process of dispersal from the villages has begun. Traditionally a country in which the popula-tion lives in large communities, some dispersal has been associated with irrigation and other reclamation schemes but in addition villagers are beginning to move out of their settlements and establish their homes on the land they till. This is particularly notable in Mexicali valley, at the head of the Gulf of California.[16]

An important question arising here is the magnitude of the benefits that may be obtained from consolidation and the share of these which may be attributed to the reduction of distances. Unfortunately, consolidation and re-location of farmsteads are usually but parts of an integrated programme, with numerous changes occurring at much the same time. Therefore, it is not possible, on the basis of accounting data collected in studies of consolidation benefits, to separate the various elements and assign each its share in improving the general well-being. However, we can get some idea of the relative magnitudes involved in the following fashion. Jacoby concluded that gross output may rise by between 20 and 70 per cent as a result of consolidation. This range may be compared with the changes which may be expected on account of a reduction in distances. To estimate this, a calculation was performed similar to that summarized in Table 16, but relating to gross and not net product. The results of this calculation indicate that a reduction in the *average* distance between the farmsteads and fields (not the distance between settlements) of half a kilometre will yield an average increase in gross product of between 6 and 7 per cent, showing that even a fairly modest rearrangement of the locations of the farmsteads can contribute appreciably to the gains obtained from consolidation. In terms of net product, the share of the benefit attributable to a reduction of the average distance is probably greater, though there is not sufficient material available to confirm this opinion. But it should be remembered that the estimates of production per hectare in relation to distance refer to conditions in which much the same techniques are applied wherever the plot is. A reduction in the average distance will have innumerable side-effects in the way of making possible methods not previously used, and so the estimate given above refers only to the direct contribution of a diminution in the average distance and, therefore, understates the benefit.

Problems of dispersal

Dispersal of the rural population does raise some awkward problems under two headings: (1) the costs of providing roads and public utilities such as electricity and water, which are greater than where everyone lives in compact settlements; (2) the loneliness which often characterizes life on isolated farms, which may be specially burdensome for those accustomed to the society of village life. Therefore, in practice it is now common for a number of compromise solutions to be attempted and a discussion of these occupies the next few paragraphs.[17]

To allow for varying degrees of soil fertility and differences in the sizes, abilities and resources of farm families, it is desirable that farms within an area should be of various sizes. In laying out an entirely new area, such as a Dutch polder, the most satisfactory arrangement of the territory, viewed solely from the farm management point of view, would be square holdings, with the farmstead located centrally. The square is the most economical shape—in the sense of minimizing the average distance from the centre to the land—that permits the whole territory to be laid out in units of varying area (see p. 123). Such a pattern of farmsteads could be provided with roads as shown in Figs. 9a and 9b (p. 139). The former requires the more costly system of roads, for it involves a maximum distance at relatively high specifications of bearing strength, etc., and likewise generous provision for services such as water and sewerage. Fig. 9b requires the same total length of roads but the spurs leading to the farms may be built more simply and the water and sewerage pipes along these spurs may be of smaller diameter. There is also a slight improvement in the ease of social intercourse but in both cases life would be isolated unless the holdings were very small. In Fig. 9c the possibilities for social intercourse are much enhanced, the cost of providing roads and public utilities is further diminished, but the farmsteads are no longer situated centrally and therefore the expenses of running the farms have been somewhat increased. If the square is abandoned (Fig. 9d), even greater economies in laying out the reclamation area can be obtained, the farmsteads can conveniently be located at one corner of the holding to form groups of four, but the farm running expenses again rise. The actual solution adopted is generally based upon Figs. 9c and 9d, and depends upon the estimates of the costs of laying out the area, balancing savings on that score against increases in the expenses of managing the farms.[18]

Modern Dutch planning is adopting the system shown in Fig. 9d, with a standard farm of 24 hectares measuring 300 metres by 800 metres, and some of the Italian reclamations made by Mussolini were also laid out in a similar fashion; on the other hand, some of the recent Italian work is based on holdings which are oblong, the shorter axis paralleling the road, each farmstead placed beside the road in the middle of the holding's frontage (cf. Fig. 9c). The same problem is manifest in some West German land consolidation schemes, where farmsteads are being re-located outside the villages in groups of three to six.

Where, as in the Dutch polders, the territory is laid out with reference to villages which provide social and shopping facilities and may also act as a collecting point for farm produce and source of farm supplies, it is desirable that so far as possible the smaller farms should be located near the village and the larger fu₋ther away. In this manner, for a given structure of farm sizes, the total costs of movement between the farms and the village will be minimized, taking the whole territory.

Another form of compromise adopted by the Dutch in recent years is to provide dwellings for wage labourers in the villages rather than on the holdings. Formerly, all the wage hands would live on or adjacent to the farm, but in the newer reclamation schemes provision is there made only for key workers such as the stockmen, who must be available at any time. The other workers are able to live in the village and therefore have readier access to the amenities of social living; perhaps equally important, their dwellings are not owned by their employer, which makes it possible for them to change jobs without forfeiting the roof over their head. For such workers, a village location provides a greater choice of readily accessible employers than would be the case with scattered residences.[19] This compromise is only possible where there is wage labour, and in Spain and Italy another solution has been essayed to meet the needs of a peasant society in which very little labour is hired. In both countries, experiments are being conducted with small residential villages where the farming fraternity live, their farms surrounding the community at no very great distance.

Thus, even at the very lowest level of the rural settlement hierarchy, the problems posed by distance have an immediate and considerable effect. It is interesting to observe that whereas at the higher levels, and primarily in connection with the spheres of influence of villages and towns, an hexagonal layout of the countryside appears to be the most appropriate in theory, this is not true at the smallest scale. This arises from the necessity of laying out the whole countryside, so that no odd unused corners are left; to do this, and at the same time provide for a variety of different farm sizes, only a few regular geometrical shapes are possible—the square, oblong, trapezium and certain triangles. The last two (trapezium and triangle) are ruled out because farm operations can be carried out most economically in fields which are rectangular and with a trapezium and triangle some fields will not be rectilinear. Hence, the best primary units are squares and oblongs, not hexagons. If one examines a map of the north-east Polder, in the Netherlands, one is immediately struck by the way in which the radial road system related to an hexagonal-type of village arrangement is modified to conform with the rectilinear needs of the farm pattern.

Concentration of settlements

So far, we have discussed various aspects of the dispersal of population from existing nucleated settlements but dispersal is not the universal trend. Where constraints of one kind or another have been removed, the spontaneous tendency has generally been for many farmsteads to be shifted from the nucleated settlements; where, locally, the constraints have become more severe, the reverse process has happened in the past and is even today occurring. A particular consideration is that of security and military requirements, especially well exemplified in Malaya and Algeria: in both countries, guerrilla activities against the established political order were aided by the dispersed distribution of the population. Hence, as a strictly military operation, the populace was forcibly gathered together into new and/ or enlarged villages. In Malaya, twelve of these villages had a population in excess of 5,000 and a further 162 had over 1,000 inhabitants. Initially, the military authorities favoured hill sites for these villages but difficulties with water supplies and the poverty of the nearby soils forced the Malayan authorities to modify policy on siting the settlements and the later ones were established on level land overlooked by defensible hills. Nevertheless, the problems of engaging in agriculture were acute and there was a sharp decline in the output of the labour intensive crops and an increase in the less intensive ones.[20] Some 0·6 million people were involved in resettlement in Malaya, compared with the even bigger programme in Algeria that affected 2·2 million souls, or 24 per cent of the Muslim population.[21]

The cultivation cost incurred with settlements as large as some of the ones in Malaya and elsewhere suggests that they are unlikely to survive long with their present populations once the military constraints are removed, unless other measures are taken deliberately to maintain the *status quo*; indeed, of the new and regrouped villages that existed in Malaya in 1954, 38 are known to have been abandoned six years later.[22] By contrast, the villages created in the Tonga Islands at the end of the eighteenth century to provide security for the inhabitants during the internecine strife which lasted into the first half of the nineteenth century have survived. After fifty years of enforced village life, peace was restored and a new allocation of lands became possible:

and although this meant travelling some distance from the house to grow food, the advantages of village life were sufficiently great to cause the village pattern to be retained . . . and this in spite of the fact that, with the years, land allocation, which may place a farm several miles from the village, has increased the inconvenience of such a settlement pattern.[23]

But if not military, then ideological considerations may operate in the same direction. In the U.S.S.R., the wish to maintain political control over the peasantry and to ensure the delivery of the prescribed quotas, together with a belief in co-operative and communal forms of organization, bespeaks the advantages of maintaining and, wherever possible, accentuating the predominantly nucleated pattern of settlement which existed prior to the Revolution. This policy has been pursued, though the effect has in practice been comparatively small and Dovring found that by 1959 the degree of concentration of the rural population was little different from what it was in 1926. One reason is that within the large territory of collective and state farms it is necessary to have subsidiary settlements so that the land may be worked efficiently; some collective farms 'have dozens of settled points within their territory'.[24] This form of organization, of a main settlement and satellite ones around, has several interesting aspects relevant to conditions in many parts of the world.

Satellite settlements

The most rudimentary manifestation of the principle is the platform which some peoples, notably shifting cultivators, erect in the midst of the growing crops to ward off the depredations of birds and animals.

The Bembas of Rhodesia keep them [the ruminants] off by putting up palings. The flights of birds which dart down on the ears of corn are driven off by shouts or volleys of stones. A network of strings is set up over the crop to enable a watchman perched on a platform to sound clappers to frighten away the birds. Certain ingenious Mois have even invented water-driven devices for making protective noises. The cultivators must often leave their villages and temporarily live near the plantation so as to keep a more effective watch. . . . Patches of cassava have the advantage of not needing such close supervision, since animals do not eat the leaves or roots of this plant. . . .[25]

Cassava's immunity makes it advantageous to grow the crops which are susceptible—e.g. millets and yams—near at hand, the cassava being placed further away where supervision is more difficult. The construction of temporary platforms becomes necessary when the relevant crops are out of view and/or earshot of the main abode, which commonly means no more than two or three hundred metres. On the other hand, fields of millet may be grown as much as 13 kilometres away, when it becomes necessary to build grass huts to accommodate the family, or a group of related families, during the crop season.

Within the economy of the Bembas are found both the watch tower for guarding the crops and the temporary, seasonally occupied encampment used to facilitate the sowing and harvesting of the crop. The world over, the latter is the more common. The inhabitants of M'saken in eastern Tunisia, an agro-town of nearly 30,000 souls of whom perhaps 10,000 are engaged in agriculture, rent land for growing wheat at distances which in extreme cases approach 100 kilometres:

Whole expeditions set out three times a year, and the men, with their teams of mules, their small tents, provisions and equipment, spend weeks at a time away from the town. They leave in the autumn to do their ploughing and sowing; then again at the beginning of the spring for weeding; and, finally, in the summer for the harvest.[26]

More surprising still is the willingness of the inhabitants of San Pedro Carcha in Guatemala to grow maize 80 kilometres away, transporting it home on their heads.[27]

Though these are extreme examples, they show the order of magnitude of distances up to which satellite settlements may exist for the purpose of crop cultivation, and there are numerous less astonishing cases. But more usual are such settlements engaged in animal husbandry as a complement to arable cultivation conducted around the main group of habitations, a system to which we have already alluded in the case of the U.S.S.R. A very common form is the arrangement subsisting in many inhabited mountain areas, in which the main settlement is located on the valley floor or on some relatively low alp: here, some crops of grain and potatoes may be grown and hay in addition. Above such a village, there are pastures which are available for grazing for but limited periods of the year and the cattle, sheep or goats are taken progressively higher as the snows recede, being again brought down as the year wanes. Since the altitudinal differences may amount to 1,000 or 2,000 metres and the horizontal distances may be several kilometres, it is convenient to establish dwellings at strategic points rather than bring the beasts down to the main village each evening. Throughout the Alps there are numerous summer villages, permanent establishments occupied only seasonally. Here, the milk is made into butter and cheese, which is taken down at periodic intervals to be sold; at the same time, provisions are brought up. In this fashion the Alpine families are regularly divided during the summer months and the subsidiary settlements form an integral part of the village economy, which would collapse without them.

Under conditions in which the population is increasing, such satellite settlements which are occupied seasonally may come to be permanently inhabited and to possess a complete economy of their own, independent of the village from which they sprang. This process has been fairly well established as a fact in England from documentary, place-name and topographical evidence, though Darby sounded a note of warning in saying that 'we do not know enough about the conditions under which the swarming-off from established villages was begun and conducted, and we cannot speculate with any certainty'.[28] What we do know indicates that after the Anglo-Saxon and Scandinavian settlement of this country, a considerable amount of waste land was still unoccupied and so remained at the time of the Norman conquest. However, before then, and up to the early fourteenth century, clearance was going on apace. This took two forms: the expansion of the cultivated territory around villages and the establishment of new settlements. Often, these were but two aspects of the same process, the relationship being most apparent in Kent. Here, the waste which surrounded each settlement provided elements essential to its economy—pannage for the pigs, timber and fuel, game and wild fruits. To exploit these resources, it was common for clearances to be made, or natural clearings sought out, where temporary huts might be built to shelter the woodcutters and swineherds. As the population increased, the arable area farmed in common had to be expanded at the expense of the hither waste, involving greater trouble in arable cultivation, wood gathering and the grazing of livestock. Thus, it frequently happened that some of the temporarily occupied clearings came to be permanently inhabited, arable cultivation began and an independent hamlet or village grew up. The suffix -den denotes a clearing which was probably used for exploiting the waste, and the Domesday Survey records a number of places in Kent with this ending to their names, distinguishing between those used only for grazing swine, those where arable land was cultivated by villeins and bordars, and, in two cases, fully independent villages—Benenden and Newenden. There are other suffixes which indicate the same process, such as *-ley* and *-field*, *-ergh* and *-booth*. The last two relate to Scandinavian colonization, meaning the summer shieling to which the cattle were taken seasonally, comparable to the Alpine summer villages; since their original foundation, they have come to be permanently inhabited.

Another important pattern of colonization—though not common in Kent—was the enclosure of land at the periphery of the village's cultivated territory. Such enclosed land was hedged and fenced and commonly the farmstead of the peasant was located on the holding. In this fashion the village, with its bare open-fields cultivated in common, might come to be surrounded by a halo of countryside privately farmed, presenting a broken-up appearance. Instead of colonization resulting in a repetition of the previous pattern, a new element was introduced into the landscape which, over the centuries, has achieved dominance, the *coup de grâce* being administered by Parliament in the hundred years from the mid-eighteenth century.[29]

A point of considerable interest is the spacing of villages in the English Midlands, where dispersed farmsteads were not generally a part of the early settlement pattern, though they have subsequently appeared on the scene. It is highly speculative to attempt to draw any conclusions on this matter, for a number of interrelated reasons. The crux of the problem is that the circumstances which led to the establishment of villages were very different from those which now exist. Generally speaking, the cultivated area did not expand to occupy the whole of a village's territory—the parish—until early in the fourteenth century, mostly several hundred years after the settlements were established or reoccupied. Furthermore, by no means all villages have survived to the present day, for many parishes have been amalgamated; alternatively, new foundations have occurred, though mostly in areas of reclamation, notably the Fens, which are of limited extent. However, if we take the present-day distribution of villages and parishes, we have a situation which corresponds fairly closely with that which had evolved by about 1300, except in a few localities. On this basis, the evidence that Beresford and St Joseph[30] summarize is relevant. Its purport is that the *minimum* distance between villages in England averages about 1·6 kilometres, which implies that the *minimum* distance to the territorial limits—the parish boundary—is about 0·8 kilometre. In which case, the average distance to the further boundaries must be greater.

To examine the matter further, by measuring the *maximum* distance from village to parish boundary, Lincolnshire was selected, as representing the range of shapes and sizes found in England and containing noticeable regional concentrations. For the county as a whole, the median distance from the named village to the *furthest* point on the parish boundary is 3·2 kilometres, or four times the *minimum* already quoted. The regional variations within the county are considerable, as is shown by Table 20. Boston, Elloe and Spalding Rural Districts contain areas of reclamation in the Fens, where the progressive intake of marshland enabled villages to extend their territory in much the same way as certain Dutch farms and certain holdings in lower Canada became very elongated. In these three Rural Districts, the maximum distance is overstated because in many parishes there is a second village; the same is true, but in lesser measure, of the other areas. South Kesteven also contains many long and thin parishes; in this case they lie transverse to the Jurassic escarpment, thereby containing a selection of all the soil types locally available, as along the north edge of the Berkshire Downs. By contrast, where the physical conditions are more nearly uniform and settlement has been long-established, the parishes are much more compact, as in Louth, which contains numerous Wolden villages.

TABLE 20

LINCOLNSHIRE: MEDIAN MAXIMUM DISTANCE FROM
NAMED VILLAGE TO PARISH BOUNDARY
(*in Kilometres*)

Rural District	Distance	Rural District	Distance
Spilsby	2·3	E. Kesteven	4·0
Grimsby	2·6	Isle of Axholme	4·2
Horncastle	2·6	S. Kesteven	4·2
Louth	2·6	Boston	5·8
Welton	3·0	Elloe	7·1
Caistor	3·2	Spalding	8·2
W. Kesteven	3·5		
Glandforde Brigg	3·5	All Lincolnshire	3·2

No very certain conclusions can be drawn from the above evidence, though it is consistent with the following proposition. In the process of crystallization into village units, the pattern which evolved and has survived is one that generally ensures a village having all its territory within a compass of 4·0 kilometres; in Lincolnshire, nearly 70 per cent of the parishes are so constituted. In the majority of cases, all the arable land would be considerably nearer and only the

E

commons and grazing would be at the further limits. Distances of this order are consonant with the evidence which has been presented earlier concerning the magnitude of economic loss associated with the cultivation of distant land, despite the very marked disparity in the levels of technical achievement between our forbears and ourselves. In the present context, the vital technical matter is the means of locomotion and the modern data mostly refer to conditions in which mechanical means of transport on the farm were not much used, so that then as now men walked with their draught animals. But even though distances were kept to reasonable proportions, the costs that they imposed were quite appreciable.

The extension of the farming area outwards from the village to its farthest limits accentuated one of the handicaps of open-field farming in a large manor, particularly if, as at Laxton, the village were not centrally placed: namely, the loss of time in getting from the homesteads to the remoter furlongs and closes, though this was not so great as sometimes represented. So, following the necessary exchanges, some of these furlongs were inclosed and withdrawn altogether from common farming . . .[31]

and new isolated settlements grew up.

The hiving-off of new settlements is not merely a process of historical interest but can be witnessed in the present day. In the former French Sudan, it is normal for each village to have its cultivated land within 1·5 or 1·8 kilometres; if the population rises, then instead of expanding the cultivated area pertaining in that village, a new settlement is founded some 2 or 3 kilometres away, bearing the same name as the parent village.[32] Nor is there a clear distinction between such a process of colonization of a permanent nature and the movement of shifting cultivators. The Iban of Sarawak are cultivators of hill rice, using a form of shifting agriculture and occupying very difficult and accidented terrain. When a new settlement is founded, the forest is cleared in the immediate vicinity and:

as long as farms lie within a radius of about half a mile to a mile (or slightly further, if they can be reached by canoe), activities are conducted from the main long-house. After a few years, however, as more distant land is brought into cultivation, accessibility becomes a problem, and when this stage is reached the community breaks up into a number of distinct groups—each group farming in a different part of the long-house territory. Typically, the whole community moves to the same general quarter of the territory. . . .[33]

A distance of between 0·8 and 1·6 kilometres represents the limiting distance at which the cost of cultivation rises high enough to warrant a shift of abode. But the long-house remains the social and business centre for the community, being occupied seasonally; after a sufficient time has elapsed for regeneration of the forest, the long-house will again be continuously inhabited for a period of years before another dispersal occurs. Thus, the hiving-off is temporary and the social links are maintained.

An interesting point is that even under adverse conditions of physical environment and poor technical accomplishments, a combination which betokens a low population density, the distance certain shifting cultivators move their main abodes is very similar to the figures which have already been quoted for normal, as against exceptional, circumstances. The Bembas of Northern Rhodesia normally choose a site on the best soils within a very few kilometres,[34] and not far away the Lala tribe was found to average 8 kilometres between the old site and the new, which implies a maximum radius of cultivation of 4 kilometres.[35]

Summary of evidence

A point which emerges from the preceding discussion and the material of Chapter 4 is the frequency with which the same orders of magnitude keep on recurring among peoples of widely different technical achievements and inhabiting areas with markedly different physical characteristics. Any distance up to about a kilometre from the dwelling is of such little moment for any but specialized systems of irrigation and garden farming that little adjustment is called for in either the pattern of settlement or of land use. Beyond about 1 kilometre, the costs of movement become sufficiently great to warrant some kind of response; at a distance of 3–4 kilometres the costs of cultivation necessitate a *radical* modification of the system of cultivation or settlement—for example by the establishment of subsidiary settlements—though adjustments are apparent before this point is reached. If the distances involved are actually greater than this, then it is necessary to look for some very powerful constraining reason which prevents the establishment of farmsteads nearer the land. Over much of the world, the present spontaneous tendency is to modify the patterns of rural settlement and land holding in such a manner that the distance separating the farmstead from the lands cultivated is reduced to something in the order of 1 or 2 kilometres, if the farmstead is not actually on the farm. Of course, there are parts of the world where this does not apply, such as the United States, Canada and Australia; these are regions of relatively recent agricultural settlement, where it was normal for the farmsteads to be placed on the holding at the time of acquisition.

Land taxation

An interesting practical application of location principles is found in the taxation of agricultural land. In those countries where it operates, the tax is levied on the assessed value of the property, which may be its market value were it sold, or the level of net income derived from its operation. In some countries, an attempt is made to assess each individual plot; this necessarily means taking account of the location of each parcel with respect to the farmstead, to arrive at the true worth—the value of the produce less the costs of cultivation. Such practices are followed in several European countries,[36] in Burma and parts of India, notably Madras and Bombay,[37] and also in the West Indies.[38] For the purpose of the assessment, the allowance which is made for location is usually arbitrary and is frequently a qualitative judgment rather than a meticulous examination of the quantitative significance of distance. Whatever the particular method used, the object is the same.

Work study

This chapter is aptly concluded with a few sentences on another practical micro-application of location principles. Work study, or time-and-motion study, is a technique which has been developed primarily by engineers, especially in connection with manufacturing industry, but the methods are now rapidly spreading to agriculture, administration and commerce.[39] The basic principle is simple: all production, assembly and distribution within a firm (factory, farm or office) requires the movement of goods and persons from point to point, or the repetition of the same sequence of operations by individual persons. Work study seeks to record and measure these movements and then to devise alternative arrangements which will reduce the total amount of movement required to achieve given objectives to the minimum that is possible. This is essentially an exercise in the relative positions of objects and the paths of movement which are traced between them in an attempt to achieve a least-cost location pattern (if the amount of production is to be constant) or a maximum profit one (if the output of the existing labour force is to be increased to the maximum).

The point is illustrated very well by a case quoted by Piel-Desruisseaux[40] in which the reorganization of a farm's buildings resulted in a saving of about 63 per cent in the *kilogramme-metres* required for their operation. In framing his analysis thus, he has set the problem squarely into Weberian terms. There is a certain type and level of production, of milk and cream in this case, for which it is necessary to perform a number of processes, such as milking the cattle. To achieve this given output, how can we arrange the layout of the buildings to minimize the amount of walking and carrying of goods? Weber measured the aggregate movement in ton-kilometres, Piel-Desruisseaux in kilogramme-metres. The farm problem is much simpler than the industrial one, since in the former case no consideration need be given to the final destination of the produce, the market. The actual results of the rearrangement of buildings are given below:

TABLE 21

REORGANIZATION OF FARM BUILDINGS
(*Thousand Kilogramme-Metres of Work Per Day*)

Commodity	Before	After
Cream	150	550
Grain	550	—
Clover, straw, silage	3,720	2,290
Whole milk	3,485	255
Separated milk	3,165	975
Total	11,070	4,070

To date, location principles have been mainly applied to particular jobs, such as the tending of cattle or the sorting of fruit. But in principle, there is no reason why work study should not encompass the spatial arrangement of the whole farm, thereby extending to the whole the logic of what is meet for the part. Indeed, although the works published in English are silent on this point, Piel-Desruisseaux is quite explicit, pointing out that the spatial arrangements of buildings, means of access and types of enterprise are closely interrelated. He advocates the advantages of having near the farm those enterprises which require much transport and further away those which require less, taking account of all operations.[41]

Some farm advisory workers in the United Kingdom are in fact already applying this principle. Imperial Chemical Industries, Ltd, provides an advisory service for farmers which has the object of

E*

raising the net income of the farms which participate. One of the means to this end is intensification of the use of the land to increase the per hectare yields, with carefully controlled rotations, grazing and management. As it is evidently not possible to effect this improvement suddenly over the whole farm, a beginning is usually made with one or two fields; the success achieved on these then provides the lessons which may be applied elsewhere on the holding. The field chosen for the initial development is always near the farmstead; as additional fields are brought into the intensive system, they form a ring round the dwelling. In time, this ring is expanded outwards to the periphery of the farm, and if it is small enough the whole area will be lifted to a higher level of productivity. Where the farm is large, it may be necessary to leave a peripheral belt which will continue to be farmed at a markedly lower level of intensity, on account of the costs of operation being too high to warrant the more intensive cultivation.[42]

BIBLIOGRAPHICAL NOTES

1. Since the rate of loss incurred becomes less as distance increases, it is not sufficient to compute the average distance for a hexagon of a given size and then assign a value for the loss on the basis of this average distance. The hexagons have been built up by adding successive belts one quarter of a kilometre broad. It was assumed that all the land in each belt did in fact lie at the average distance for that belt. For each belt, a figure could then be assigned for the loss of net product, and in this manner a weighted average loss was obtained for hexagons of the desired size. A selection of the figures which were used for this calculation is shown below:

Distance in kms.	Net product as per cent	Distance in kms.	Net product as per cent
0–0·1	100	2·0	54
0·5	86	3·0	42
1·0	73	4·0	35
1·5	63		

2. G. Barbero, *Land reform in Italy: achievements and perspectives*, F.A.O., *Agricultural Studies*, no. 53, 1961: *Annuario dell'Agricoltura Italiana*, 1963, p. 130 of the appendix and 1965, p. 190.

3. *Informazioni SVIMEZ*, April 12–19, 1950, pp. 221–4.

4. G. E. Marciani, *L'Esperienza di Riforma Agraria in Italia*, 1966, pp. 145–6.

5. E. H. Jacoby, *Land Consolidation in Europe*, International Institute for Land Reclamation and Improvement, publication 3/E, 1959, p. 13. Agricultural areas from F.A.O., *Production Yearbook*, 1958, p. 3. See also: A. M. Lambert, 'Farm consolidation in Western Europe', *Geography*, 1963, 31–48.

6. H. Thorpe, 'The influence of inclosure on the form and pattern of rural settlement in Denmark', *Transactions and Papers*, Institute of British Geographers, 1951, pp. 113–28.

7. N. Gubsky, 'The land settlement of Russia', *Economic Journal*, 1921, p. 475.

8. The information contained in the previous two paragraphs is based upon Jacoby, 1959, *supra*.

9. K. Skovgard, 'Consolidation of agricultural land in Denmark', in *The Consolidation of Fragmented Agricultural Holdings*, B. O. Binns, F.A.O., *Agricultural Studies*, No. 11, 1953, pp. 41–55; F. Skrubbeltrang, *Agricultural Development and Rural Reform in Denmark*, F.A.O., *Agricultural Studies*, No. 22, 1953, pp. 7–73.

10. W. G. Hoskins, *The Making of the English Landscape*, 1955, pp. 157 and 159.

11. For example, see W. H. R. Curtler, *The Enclosure and Redistribution of our Land*, 1920; E. K. C. Gonner, *Common Land and Inclosure*, 1912; A. H. Johnson, *The Disappearance of the Small Landowner*, 1909; or any standard economic history of the United Kingdom.

12. J. D. Chambers, 'Enclosure and labour supply in the industrial revolution', *Economic History Review*, Ser. II, Vol. V, 1952–3, pp. 319–43.

13. E. Schuler, 'Untersuchungen über verbundene Flurbereinigungs und Assiedlungsverfahren in Baden-Wurttemberg', *Schriftenreihe für Flurbereinigung*, West German Federal Ministry of Food, Agriculture and Forestry, 1957, pp. 59 and 75.

14. A. Demangeon, *Problèmes de Géographie Humaine*, 3rd edn., 1947, pp. 366–8; *Annales de Géographie*, 1926, pp. 155–73.

15. J. E. de Young, *Village Life in Modern Thailand*, 1955, pp. 10–11.

16. N. L. Whetten, *Rural Mexico*, 1948, p. 44.

17. A. P. Takes, 1958, *supra* (ch. 4).

18. C. P. Barnes, 'The economics of the long-lot farm', *Geographical Review*, 1935, pp. 298–301.

19. A. K. Constandse, 'L'aménagement d'un polder aux Pays-Bas: problèmes sociaux et démographiques', *Population*, 1957, pp. 401–12.

20. K. S. Sandhu, 'Emergency resettlement in Malaya', *Journal of Tropical Geography*, August 1964, pp. 157–83.

21. M. Lesne, 'Une expérience de déplacement de population: les centres de regroupement en Algérie', *Annales de Géographie*, 1962, pp. 567–603.

22. Sandhu, 1964, *supra*, p. 166.

23. T. F. Kennedy, 'Village settlement in Tonga', *New Zealand Geographer*, 1958, pp. 164–5.

24. Dovring, 1965, *supra* (ch. 4), p. 18.

25. A. I. Richards, 'A changing pattern of agriculture in East Africa: the Bemba of Northern Rhodesia', *Geographical Journal*, 1958, p. 307.

26. R. Dumont, *Types of Rural Economy*, English edn., 1957, pp. 178–9.

27. P. Gourou, *The Tropical World*, 2nd English edn., 1958, p. 50.

28. H. C. Darby, 'The economic geography of England, A.D. 1000–1250', in H. C. Darby (Ed.), *Historical Geography of England before 1800*, 1936, p. 182.

29. Hoskins, 1955, *supra*; Darby, 1936, *supra*; M. W. Beresford and J. K. S. St Joseph, *Medieval England: an Aerial Survey*, 1958; R. Lennard, 1959, *supra* (ch. 6).

30. Beresford and St Joseph, 1958, *supra*.

31. Orwin and Orwin, 1954, *supra* (ch. 6), p. 162.

32. P. V. de la Blache, *Principles of Human Geography*, English edn., 1926, pp. 58–9.

33. J. D. Freeman, *Iban Agriculture: a Report on the Shifting Cultivation of Hill Rice by the Iban of Sarawak*, Colonial Research Studies, no. 18, 1955, p. 33.

34. Richards, 1958, *supra*, p. 307.

35. D. U. Peters, 'Land usage in the Serenje District', *Rhodes-Livingstone Papers*, no. 19, 1950, p. 51.

36. J. P. van Aartsen, 'Land classification in relation to its agricultural value: a review of systems applied', *International Review of Agriculture*, July–August 1944, p. 79S; November–December 1944, p. 139S.

37. H. P. Wald, *Taxation of Agricultural Lands in Underdeveloped Economies*, 1959.

38. E. Paget, 'Value, valuation and use of land in the West Indies', *Geographical Journal*, 1961, pp. 493–8.

39. For a history of work study, see M. N. Tcherkinsky, *L'Organisation Scientifique du Travail Agricole en Europe*, 1931.

40. Piel-Desruisseaux, *supra* (ch. 4), p. vi–5.

41. For other literature on work study, see B. Branston, *Time and Motion on the Farm*, 1952; N. Harvey, *Farm Work Study*, 1958; A. K. Fraser and G. W. Lugg, *Work Study in Agriculture*, 1962.

42. Conversation with Mr J. Clark, Imperial Chemical Industries Ltd.

8

THE REGION AND THE WORLD: II

This chapter falls into two parts of unequal length. The first and longer section is concerned with the relatively simple but neglected problem of the location of lines of communication with respect to rural and urban needs or potential needs. The second part is designed to round off the picture by showing that the explanation for differing densities of rural population in the various parts of the world requires one step of argument which places the discussion into the locational framework that is being developed in this book.

Location of a transport route

We have seen that in considering the destination of produce and the source of inputs, remembering the various stages of marketing, it is desirable to include not only inhabited centres, which may be treated as points, but also traffic arteries. These may be regarded as continuous lines, even though access to them is limited to relatively few specified places. An important problem arises each time there is a proposal to build a new route, be it of whatever kind, i.e., where shall it be located? Many consequences turn upon the answer, among them the profitability of the transport enterprise, the effectiveness of the transport service to be provided, changes in land use and production and the development of urban centres. In a limited number of cases, there is no effective choice between routes because the costs incurred in using any but the 'obvious' one would be too great. To connect New York by canal with the Great Lakes by any means other than the Hudson-Mohawk alignment would have involved enormous additional expenses which could easily be recognized and which would have yielded no return. Or if a road is to be built between Fort William and Inverness, how otherwise could it be aligned than along the Great Glen? But in the generality of cases, there is a greater choice and consequently a nice problem of location is presented.

Imagine a private investor interested in building a railway. He will be concerned with a number of closely related questions, some of which may be summarized thus:

(1) Will the amount of traffic obtainable between A and B provide enough revenue to meet the expenses of operating the line and to yield a reasonable return on the capital invested?

(2) What route between A and B will serve to maximize the total net receipts derived from traffic between A and B and that originating from or destined to points lying between A and B?

(3) Would a line built between any other two places, X and Y, be more profitable?

If, instead of a private individual, it were a government or other public body contemplating a new venture, the fundamental questions would be the same, though the phrasing might be different: which route will enable the maximum amount of transport to be provided for a given allocation of funds?

The principle which underlies the answer to these questions is simple, though the practical application of it is fraught with great difficulties and uncertainties. The basic aim will be to situate the railway where the amount of actual or potential traffic which may be tapped per route kilometre is at a maximum. This is subject to the reservation that, in choosing a route which maximizes the traffic per unit distance of track, the construction and running costs are not raised unduly; if they are, then a compromise solution must be sought. For example, the shorter of alternative alignments may tap a greater amount of traffic per kilometre of way, but involve steep gradients and curves of small radius which raise construction costs and running expenses to such a level that the longer route proves to be more advantageous.

A simple example may be taken to illustrate the matter. Suppose that it is intended to build a railway through a strip of territory some 5 kilometres broad, comprising a level plain in which the land is disposed in five bands running parallel with the general direction of the railway. The land outside this swathe of 5 kilometres is quite uncultivated; within it, the five bands are disposed as in Fig. 10. Band A represents the best quality of soil for farming, C and C_1 the

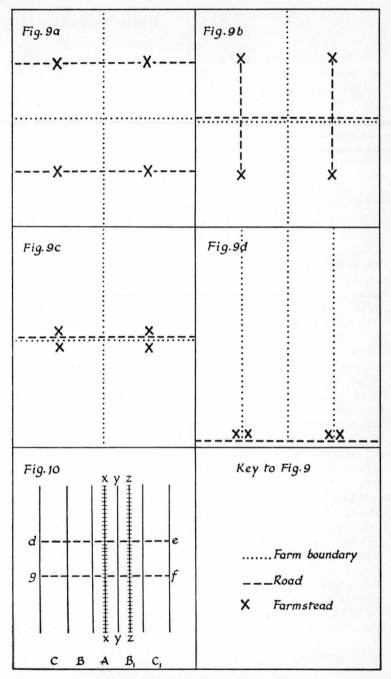

Fig. 9a

Fig. 9b

Fig. 9c

Fig. 9d

Fig. 10

x y z

d — — — — — — — e

g — — — — — — — f

x y z

C   B   A   B₁   C₁

Key to Fig. 9

.... Farm boundary

— — — Road

X   Farmstead

Fig. 9   Rural road patterns (see p. 122)
Fig. 10   Location of a single route (see p. 138)

poorest, while B and B_1 are intermediate in fertility. The consequence of these differing degrees of fertility is that the total produce of a square kilometre plus the requisite inputs of fertilizer, etc., amounts to 1,000 metric tons annually for the best land, 750 and 500 respectively for the intermediate and worst soil. We will further suppose that access to the railway is possible at all points. Then, since we may assume that the costs of constructing and running the railway are not affected by the alignment which is chosen within the belt of territory, the problem of location resolves itself into that which will minimize the cost of getting goods to and from the line, which is to minimize the ton-kilometres required.

Let the first choice of alignment be XX, and consider then a segment of territory defg measuring 5 kilometres by 1. If the average distance from the railway to each of the three categories of land is multiplied by the tonnage of goods to be taken to and from the line, it will be found that the ton-kilometres required for access to the railway amount to 3,750 each year. Should the route YY be chosen, the figure would be 3,960, while ZZ would entail a total of 4,687 ton-kilometres; any more eccentric position would involve even greater costs of access to the route. In this hypothetical case, the optimum location is XX and any deviation from XX results in additional and unnecessary expenses.

It may be that all of these expenses of movement to and from the railway are borne by persons other than the railway company, in which case the above analysis leaves the investor indifferent as to the route chosen. But this is only because we have assumed that the amount of traffic relating to each plot of land is unaffected by its distance from the railway. Such an assumption is clearly contrary to the evidence which has already been presented and is amply disproved by the work of Zipf and Isard.[1] These authors have shown that for a wide range of activities the amount of intercourse and interchange declines with marked regularity as distance increases. The actual relationship is of course variable but the order of magnitude is often given as the inverse relation of distance or of the square of distance or some intermediate value. Thus, if we regard the hypothetical figures of tons per hectare as only applying to land if it is immediately adjacent to the railway, some discount must be made for distance away from it. If this is done, it follows that removing the railway from the alignment XX to some other, such as YY, has the effect of reducing the amount of traffic which will be offered. This would result in an unnecessary loss of business for the company and therefore makes it advantageous to choose the central alignment.

For the purpose of exposition, a simple case has been selected but the principle is applicable generally. Wherever there is territory which varies in its capacity to generate traffic, it will normally be advantageous to locate a new route as close as possible to those areas which actually do, or potentially will, give rise to the most business. Exactly the same is true of improvements to existing facilities: where there is a choice of projects, it is a better economic proposition to renovate or replace where existing traffic demand is greatest, rather than in the less congested areas (see p. 145).

In practice, although the greater part of a communications system usually lies in rural areas, the basic layout of the network is generally more influenced by urban and industrial needs than by rural and agricultural requirements. Therefore, it is hardly relevant to discuss the problem of where to locate a new route other than in the context of the economy as a whole, though the principles which are involved are identical to those outlined above. The matter was treated at considerable length by Wellington,[2] an engineer who was responsible for planning the location of the Mexican railways. Two of his observations are specially relevant. He estimated that the adverse effect upon gross revenue of placing a station away from the centre of a town amounted to a reduction of 10 per cent for each 1·6 kilometres in the case of a small country town without a competitive alternative and 25 per cent for large industrial cities possessing competing railway facilities. This is an effect analogous to the smaller amount of traffic which will be generated by a plot of agricultural land the further removed it is from the railway. Second, he considered that if a line were going to be built between two points, and if all intermediate points were of equal traffic generating capacity and were equally spaced, then the amount of traffic on the line would vary as the square of the number of these points served. This then justifies quite considerable detours to link up such sources of traffic.

Wellington was writing at a time when modern road transport had yet to be developed and therefore when movement tributary to a railway was more difficult than it now is; therefore, his empirical values are probably no longer valid for new construction, but they were eminently important when much of the present-day network of the world was being built.

The fundamental proposition which has been made above, that if conditions of the physical environment and economic development are known and the construction of a new transport artery or system is contemplated, then the layout of communications is the variable factor, finds its application in the study of Bourrières.[3] From the production data available, he calculated the value of output per square kilometre in the different parts of the Ivory Coast and found that it was highest in the southern forest zone, lowest in the north and intermediate in the savanna areas. On this basis, his recommendations envisaged the densest network of road and rail routes in the forest regions, the sparsest network in the further interior. These recommendations accorded with the then existing relative densities of the communication systems in the different parts of the country.

Another excellent example is provided by the survey carried out for a proposed extension of the Nigerian railway network to Maiduguri in the extreme north-east.[4] Ultimately, five possible alignments were considered, three starting at Lafia, one at Kuru and one at Bukuru, all stations on the north-south route which crosses the Jos Plateau. The north-east of Nigeria is an under-developed region, largely on account of the poor transport facilities, and the survey was conducted to determine which route through the territory would be the most profitable. An investigation was made as to the existing and potential levels of agricultural production available for evacuation, return goods traffic and passenger movements in the different parts of the area. Account was taken of the actual and prospective competition from other transport media and probable diversions of traffic from existing rail routes to the possible new ones. From such data, the prospective revenue from each section of line was estimated and compared with the expected capital and running expenses. The report which resulted from these investigations unequivocally recommended that the most advantageous route was from Kuru to Maiduguri via Bauchi and Gombe. This had the advantage of being short, traversing the more fertile regions, serving the important consuming area of the Jos Plateau and avoiding the necessity for heavy compensation for the loss of mining rights involved in the Bukuru proposal. Though this report illustrates admirably the locational principles involved in planning a transport route, and though it is probable that the best alignment was chosen for the construction of the extension, by the time the line was opened to traffic in 1964 improvements in road transport facilities had made it unlikely that the railway extension would be profitable.

The case may be clinched by even a cursory glance at the history of railway development in the United Kingdom, though in so doing we are digressing somewhat from immediately rural matters. The railways were built by private companies which had obtained parliamentary consent for the particular route; amalgamations also had to be sanctioned by an Act. Thus, fortunes were made and lost in a battle conducted at the political and financial level: political, because votes in Parliament had to be wooed and won; financial, because money had to be enticed into bonds. It was also an economic battle between the railways and the canals and roads, and between competing railway companies. If there were three kinds of move—political, financial and economic—available to the promoters of new lines or of amalgamations, there was only one arena—a chessboard of locations. Recurrent themes therefore emerge.

First, the earliest routes to be built were those where there was an already existing demand for transport facilities, particularly for the movement of coal:

The chief reason why the railways came into existence was because of the need of more adequate facilities for conveyance than the canals could give. The enormous profits which some canals were making were also an inducement for railways to come in and secure a share of these benefits, and the success of existing railroads, giving additional encouragement to the projectors of new lines, had an important effect in initiating these enterprises along routes where they were much needed.[5]

After the opening of the Stockton–Darlington line in 1825, to supply an existing need for mineral transport—a canal had been projected for the same purpose—the next major lines were all built by local interests to break canal monopolies: Liverpool–Manchester, Liverpool–Birmingham, Birmingham–London, London–Bristol. The succeeding projects which actually materialized were to connect existing centres between which much traffic already flowed, for example Newcastle–Carlisle, London–Southampton and Leeds–Hull. An examination of the railway network at 1840 and 1850, as given by Wilfred Smith,[6] shows quite clearly how the first lines linked up centres which generated a lot of traffic.

Second, if occasionally the early lines were built where there was little previous traffic movement, it was because the promoters anticipated a good potential of trade, hopes which were not always realized.

Third, the battles to obtain concessions for routes, to reach working agreements with, and to take over, other companies, were fundamentally struggles to control lucrative traffic. Though political, financial and managerial skills were requisite, these would avail nothing if the company chose a poor route to operate or was subsequently outmanœuvred in the locational struggle. The two stations possessed by many towns in England, such as Reading, Nottingham and Leicester, is a current testimony to the attempts made to secure traffic and drive out competitors in an effort to develop and maintain regional monopolies such as that achieved by the North Eastern in the area between Berwick, Hull and the Pennine foothills. Gloucester was one of the early strategic prizes, for when the Great Western linked this city to its line from London, any possible incursion of Midland companies into the south-west was effectively barred and at the same time the Great Western gained access to South Wales, enabling it to project and ultimately complete a line to Fishguard to capture much of the Irish trade.[7]

Exactly the same kind of drama has been enacted upon the American stage. In the period after the depression of 1884:

> The strife between railroad systems in the West became more virulent and was the force behind an increasing proportion of railroad construction. Within a few years three new routes were completed between Chicago and Kansas City. One was by the Atchison, Topeka & Santa Fè to strengthen its bargaining power with its eastern connections, another by the Chicago, Milwaukee & St Paul to increase its control of western traffic, and a third by one of the predecessors of the present Minneapolis & St Louis.[8]

There can be no doubt that the early history of the railways in the United Kingdom, United States and elsewhere was of competition, with the object of establishing local and regional monopolies, taking place within a matrix of alternative locations, each offering different advantages. Success depended in part upon the skill with which these advantages were evaluated. A full understanding of railway history cannot be obtained unless the events are viewed as an exercise in the practical economics of location, as is amply demonstrated by Grodinsky in his study of railway development in the United States.[9] Furthermore, such knowledge facilitates an understanding of the present-day problems of mergers between companies and the reduction in the size of the network that are a feature of many developed states.

The above discussion has been based on the assumption that the new traffic artery is to be a railway, but this assumption derives solely from the fact that the documentation for railways is much more complete than for other media of transport. Exactly the same considerations apply to all other forms of transport, by land, sea or air. That this is the case may be seen from the basic plan for the construction of modern motorways in Great Britain. These new roads are to be laid out in the form of an H, with a narrow waist centred on Birmingham–Coventry and limbs extending to London, Exeter, Penrith and Doncaster (for York). The figure will be completed by east-west links in the north and south, from near Manchester to east of Leeds and between Newport and London. The first major section of this system, the M1 opened in 1959, forms part of the London–York route. Even a quick look at the map will show that this basic layout links up the major conurbations along routes with a heavy existing load of traffic. Indeed, the plans made by the Ministry of Transport are based upon traffic surveys designed to establish the pattern of current need and are intended to relieve the worst congestion between cities.

Improved transport services

So much for the provision of new routes. Similar considerations apply to the organization of new or improved services on existing routes: the innovation tends to be first applied in areas where the existing demand is high, spreading into the less-rewarding regions at a later date. This has been clearly demonstrated in the case of omnibus services in Sweden. Godlund[10] prepared maps of the routes served at selected years back to 1915 and in one case 1907. It is quite apparent how the first country routes to be exploited were those radiating from and connecting the more important centres and that the remoter and smaller places generating less traffic were brought into the system at a later date. Nor is the reason far to seek, for analysis of the financial returns showed a high positive correlation with the density of population in the territory served: the sparser the population, the lower the returns per vehicle-kilometre and vice versa. This is similar to the finding that milk collection costs are higher in areas of England and Wales in which but little milk is produced and lower where output is concentrated (Chapter 6).

In his study of Wiltshire, Bracey was struck by the:

comprehensive development and high frequency of bus services in the valleys converging on Salisbury, in spite of the relatively low overall population density of Downland Wiltshire. These high frequencies have been encouraged by the linear settlement pattern, which offers a higher total population per 'bus mile' than obtains under less concentrated settlement.[11]

Indeed, the annual reports of British omnibus operators for the last few years present a recurrent theme: as Parliament, through the agency of the Licensing Authorities, insists on the maintenance of rural services which make a loss, some form of concessions in fuel and/or vehicle taxation ought, it is claimed, to be granted to enable the companies to make a 'reasonable' profit.

It will not have escaped the reader's attention that the above argument is nothing but the following proposition: that an area which is initially favoured, for whatever reason, tends to obtain the best communications first, which helps to reinforce the pre-existing relative advantage possessed by that region. In fact the analysis developed by Weber, Hoover, Lösch and Isard, leading to the conclusion that agglomeration of urban-industrial activity is a proper and normal occurrence, also has its application in rural matters. Furthermore, there is an important element in the general case which appears to have been overlooked or not to have received the attention which it deserves. As far as it has been taken by Isard, the analysis which leads to the conclusion that the agglomeration of economic activity is the normal phenomenon is based upon the assumption that no innovation is introduced into a situation where techniques are assumed to remain constant. The conclusion is reinforced when account is taken of the factor discussed in the last few paragraphs, that an innovation in transport techniques tends to be first employed where there is already a high level of economic development and consequently a big demand for transport services. As new techniques are being developed at relatively frequent intervals, the main agglomerations tend to enjoy a succession of advantages and this must be a factor of some importance in maintaining the advantages of existing urban concentrations.

Further discussion of the agglomeration of agricultural settlements and land uses is reserved to the next chapter. To complete this one, a few remarks are warranted on the world distribution of rural population. These comments are not intended to elicit new facts or theories on the causes of high and low densities, but rather to point out that an important step in the argument which is commonly just assumed, and is hence little remarked, fits into the pattern of analysis developed in this book.

World distribution of rural population

There are many parts of the world in which a dense peasant population following a largely self-sufficient way of life has come into
existence—the riverine lands of the lower Yangtze or Indus, for
example. That such densities should be possible may be ascribed to
many factors but the most important set of considerations is that
with the existing techniques employed these areas offer the possibility
of high yields on a sustained basis. Whereas a southern Japanese
farming family may be able to live on the produce of less than one
hectare of lowland soil, such a feat would be unthinkable in the
mountainous interior of Hokkaido in the north, owing to the lower
inherent fertility of these boreal lands.

Such reasoning is not complete. It states only that the more fertile
lands are capable of *supporting* more persons per hectare of cultivated soil and says nothing as to *where* these people live. We have
already seen (Chapter 4) that in certain circumstances agriculturalists
live many kilometres from the lands which they regularly cultivate.
Hence, it is conceivable that a Japanese family owning some fertile
lowland patch might choose to live where the climate was pleasanter
or the view more beautiful. Should sufficient families do just this,
the paradoxical position would arise in which the more fertile area
was the less densely peopled, though providing sustenance for persons
living elsewhere. In a peasant society, this does not occur on anything but a local scale: defence against enemies, for example, is an
important reason for villages being located on hilltops near the
cultivated land. At the regional and world scale, it does not happen,
for the reason that the prospective costs would be so enormous as
to be insupportable. We have seen the handicap which is imposed
by even 4 kilometres separating dwelling and field: distances much
greater than this would mean such a deterioration of the productivity
of both land and labour that it would be impossible to maintain
existing populations with the techniques which they currently employ.
The disadvantages of separation are multiplied enormously where it
is necessary to guard crops against predatory beasts and birds, as in
Africa and jungle areas generally, and where irrigation is practised
or livestock kept.

The relationship between the capacity of the soil and the density
of the population actually living on it operates only through the costs
of separation, which are too great to be tolerated. Obvious, yes. But
once stated, it is evident that in fact any analysis of the distribution
of population in subsistence-type economies is an exercise in

location concerned with the effects of the cost of overcoming distance.

Scale of farm enterprise

When considering populations engaging partially or completely in an exchange economy, the consideration discussed above must be taken in conjunction with access to markets and the availability of inputs such as machinery and fertilizers. In large measure, this brings us back to the analysis which has already been developed. But in the context of regional differences in population density it is opportune to note the part played by the scale of operations, or the size of the farm enterprise. This has so far been largely ignored as being relatively unimportant and certainly when considering agriculture the economies which arise from larger scales of operation are much less marked than in many industrial and commercial pursuits. There are three kinds of scale economy which are particularly important in operating a farm: in buying farm requisites, in selling the produce and in managing the farm. The first two types of economy can be secured by having a large farm or by the organization of co-operatives for trading purposes. By pooling their trading, a number of small farms can secure the economies available to large traders, such as discounts on bulk orders. The third type of economy, of managing the farm, can also be secured in part by small operators; for example, by the joint or co-operative ownership of pieces of equipment such as combine harvesters and by hiring the services of contract firms to perform particular operations. A case of the latter is the growing practice of contracting for the spraying of crops. Thus, although there are economies to be had from large-scale operations, it is not essential that there be large farms to obtain them.

Although the scale consideration is relatively unimportant in agriculture compared with other industries, nevertheless the size of farm does have some influence on the type and intensity of land use and the density of rural population. Other things being equal, the smaller a farm is the more intensively it is cultivated. This arises from the fact that in practice the ordinary farmer does not seek to obtain the maximum income he can, but rather attempts to achieve a standard of living which he regards as reasonable: once this is attained, leisure becomes increasingly valuable and the farmer is inclined to refrain from achieving a maximum income in order to have time off from work. The smaller the farm, the greater must be the net income per hectare even to achieve a reasonable minimum standard of living: there is, then, a strong tendency to apply more labour and other inputs to each hectare than on larger farms. In pursuit of this aim, the farmer may choose more intensive products such as poultry or glasshouse tomatoes in preference to less intensive items like wheat and potatoes.

In this fashion, an area may support a denser population than might otherwise be the case, albeit probably at a lower standard of living. Underlying this consideration of farm size is the question of the mobility of the farm population. If persons were able to move freely from one area to another and from one occupation to another and the whole economy adjusted smoothly to each change in whatever quarter, then the regional size of farm would be a *consequence* of the physical conditions of the area, the location with respect to markets and sources of inputs, the level of techniques employed and the availability of alternative non-farm employment. These would determine the types of products and the intensity of land use, which in turn would determine the size of farm capable of yielding an acceptable living income.

Most populations are, in greater or lesser degree, immobile, finding changes in geographical location and/or employment difficult. Under these circumstances, a change in the number of inhabitants will have an immediate effect upon the size of farms in the area concerned. With an increasing populace, there will be strong pressure for the division of holdings and a general intensification of output. In such a case, it is not the size of farm which is the cause of the type and intensity of agriculture; both are consequences of a more basic factor, the increase of population.

The question of farm size is therefore intimately bound up with a whole host of interrelated causes and is not normally an independent causal factor at the regional and world scales. An exception is when legislative action is taken decreeing the maximum or minimum size a holding may be, or instituting a tax which serves to encourage larger or smaller properties. Yugoslavia has a law that no one may own more than 10 hectares of productive land, while in many schemes of land consolidation elsewhere a prohibition is placed on any subsequent division of the holding. At least one of the Australian states legislated during the last century for a differential tax on land, the larger holdings paying proportionately more as an inducement to split them up into smaller units. The overt intention was to encourage denser settlement.

Clearly, in the normal course of events, farm size is not an important independent factor in the present context, and it is justifiable to ignore the matter.

BIBLIOGRAPHICAL NOTES

1. Zipf, 1949, *supra* (ch. 5); Isard, 1956, *supra* (ch. 1).

2. A. M. Wellington, *The Economic Theory of the Location of Railways*, 6th edn., 1898.

3. Bourrières, 1950, *supra* (ch. 3).

4. K. L. Crawford, for Nigerian Railway Corporation, *Bauchi-Bornu Railway Extensions: Supplementary Traffic Survey Report*, 1956.

5. W. T. Jackman, *The Development of Transportation in Modern England*, Vol. 2, 1916, p. 514.

6. W. Smith, *An Economic Geography of Great Britain*, 2nd edn., 1953, p. 161.

7. Jackman, 1916, *supra*; C. E. R. Sherrington, *The Economics of Rail Transport in Great Britain*, 1928; J. H. Clapham, *An Economic History of Modern Britain* (*The Early Railway Age*, 1926, and *Free Trade and Steel*, 1932); H. Ellis, *British Railway History*, Vol. I, 1954, Vol. II, 1959.

8. K. T. Healy, *The Economics of Transportation in America*, 1940, p. 12; also, W. Z. Ripley, *Railroads: Finance and Organization*, 1915.

9. J. Grodinsky, *Transcontinental Railway Strategy, 1869–1893: A Study of Businessmen*, 1962.

10. S. Godlund, *Bus Service in Sweden*, Lund Studies in Geography, Ser B., Human Geography, No. 17, 1956.

11. H. E. Bracey, *Social Provision in Rural Wiltshire*, 1952, p. 16.

9

TECHNICAL CHANGE

So far, the question of technical change has received only incidental notice. The method adopted in the previous chapters has been to consider situations in which, at the relevant time, the technical equipment employed was assumed to be unchanging. The idea of development has been conveyed mainly by the examination of a sequence of cases, each study relating to a point in time later than the previous one, as in Chapter 5. In this way, a number of the more obvious consequences of developments in transport and related techniques have been brought to light, notably the enlargement of the supply areas for the major urban concentrations of population.

The purpose of this chapter is to draw together some of these threads and by working systematically to attempt to weave some additional designs. In so doing, attention will be directed mainly to what is happening at present and, where appropriate, an attempt will be made to indicate the significance of trends for the future. This venture risks the possibility that events may not take the course which has been charted for them. There are two defences against this eventuality. First, every effort has been made to be judicious. Second, indiscretion may, I believe, be forgiven on the following grounds. Theoretical analysis and study of the past and present may be justified for their own sake in the pursuit of knowledge. Where the findings have implications relevant to decisions which must be taken in the present or future, or merely for understanding what is happening and is likely to happen, then it is unsatisfactory to call a halt to the investigations, leaving it to others to make the predictions. The logic of the case which has been made in the previous chapters requires some glance at present and probable future trends.

To avoid possible confusion, it should be noted that the discussion below relates to the economically developed countries rather than the so-called under-developed ones. Thus, the analysis which is developed does not claim universal validity, though it seems likely that events happening in the United States and western Europe now will find close parallels in the less advanced countries in future decades—or maybe generations. We begin with a discussion of technical changes affecting the farm and village scale of phenomenon and then proceed to regional and world matters.

Improved transport on the farm

The most striking innovation on the farm regarding modes of transport in recent decades has been the tractor. First developed as a wheeled vehicle, the later introduction of track-laying or crawler tractors considerably widened the range of applications as a source of power for farming operations on sloping and heavy lands. The wheeled vehicles in particular achieve relatively high speeds, which is invaluable for carting goods from one place to another. The rapid growth of the tractor fleet of the world, excluding the U.S.S.R., is shown by the fact that in 1938–9 there were 3·6 million vehicles, and in 1964 11·4 million, over three times the number and individually more powerful. At the same time, the number of horses, mules and asses—the chief draught animals—has been falling, from 125·0 million in 1938–9 to 110·3 million in 1964–5.[1]

Parts of Europe and North America have already very largely replaced animal power with mechanical means and in some countries, such as Great Britain, further increase in tractor numbers can only occur if the cultivated area is extended or if individual farms add to the number which they own. Over much of the rest of the world, there is a long way to go in replacing draught animal and human power by tractors. A rough measure of this is given by Table 22, which shows the number of hectares of arable land and permanent grass in relation to the 1954 and 1964 stocks of agricultural tractors. It would be wrong to suppose that ultimately the whole world will reach the position of Europe and North America, for farming conditions vary enormously. For example, it is only recently that small machines have been developed suitable for use in Japanese paddy lands and it seems unlikely that tractors could ever be as important

TABLE 22

WORLD, 1954 AND 1964: TRACTORS IN RELATION TO
AGRICULTURAL AREA

Region	Area in arable and permanent grass, million hectares 1964	Hectares of arable and permanent grass per agricultural tractor	
		1954	1964
Europe	242	141	51
North and Central America	629	127	118
U.S.S.R.	600	—	390
South America	386	2,724	1,008
Oceania	495	1,641	1,282
Africa	896	5,945	3,570
Asia	842	13,108	2,673

Source: F.A.O. *Production Yearbook.*

in terraced rice cultivation as in wheat production on the prairies and pampas.

More modest technical improvements can also have an enormous effect. Such may be the replacement of head porterage by mule or donkey, the use of a proper harness in place of the clumsy yoking of oxen by their horns, the employment of the faster horse instead of the lumbering ox, or the provision of inflatable rubber tyres instead of the metal rims on wooden wheels common to many carts. Nor is it necessary to travel outside Europe to find areas where such innovations could be of great benefit. Early in the 1950s in the Italian commune of Borgo a Mozzano, remote in the mountains between Florence and Lucca, 95 per cent of goods were moved by human porterage and pack mules.[2] Universally in the poorer parts of southern Europe, oxen yoked by the horns draw clumsy, solid-wheeled carts.

In contrast to these modest improvements, the application of aerial methods to many agricultural operations catches the imagination. Since the last world war, there has been a spectacular increase in such activities, including spraying, dressing, seeding, dropping rabbit poison in New Zealand and facilitating fence construction in otherwise inaccessible areas. In the short span of fifteen years, the area treated by aerial means in the United States rose from almost 16 million hectares in 1951 to just over 30 million in 1957 and 97 million in 1966.[3] Such has been the growth of this new technique

F

that there is now a European Agricultural Aviation Centre at The Hague, issuing a quarterly journal. Undoubtedly aerial techniques are going to be of growing importance to farmers all over the world.

Apart from improvements to the means of transport within the farm, it is important to notice also the development of devices for transport saving. This is closely related to the matter of work study, which has been discussed in Chapter 7. An example is the design of yards so that cattle can feed from silage without the latter having to be cut and carted, or self-feeding, as it is called. Another method is the use of mobile milking units which can be placed in the fields, reducing the amount of walking required of the cattle.

It is not possible to assess the total effect of these and other innovations in diminishing the amount and cost of movement within the individual farm and to compare these savings with the economies in production achieved by other means. But it seems safe to aver that the benefits have been sufficiently great in relation to other developments, such as increases in yields, for the problem of transport within the farm to have declined in relative importance in the more advanced countries. It would appear that this decline will continue, if for no other reason than the prospective growth of aerial operations. In the less developed countries, a substantial drop in the relative cost of transport may be expected merely from the adoption of known techniques which are not at present widely used there. This relative decline in the importance of transport would seem to be likely even despite the spectacular increases in yields which can be obtained in some parts of the world from the application of simple devices like nitrogenous fertilizers: if yields rise three or four fold, production expenses per unit of output do not decline in like measure because the fertilizer itself has to be bought and a considerable amount of additional labour is required to cope with the extra cultivation and the bigger harvest to be gathered, while it may be necessary to provide additional storage facilities.

External relations of settlements

When it comes to local transport external to the farm, the story is the same. The substitution of bicycles, motor-bicycles, cars and lorries for more primitive methods has meant, or promises to mean, a substantial decline in the relative cost of transport. This proposition is more aptly documented later in the context of the regional and world scales of consideration and only two points will be mentioned now.

Enormously important is the increase in personal mobility conferred by the possession of a bicycle or motor vehicle, which enables rural workers to live several kilometres or more from the place of work. The proportion of persons owning such means of locomotion is rising and undoubtedly will continue to rise, principally on account of improvements in the standard of living. Second and often overlooked is the fact that working hours are getting shorter in many parts of the world, with the consequence:

(1) That people have more time in which to travel, and

(2) Have more leisure to occupy, and hence greater social needs, which encourages them to travel daily so that once at home these needs may be fulfilled.

At the same time as social needs are increasing, the capacity to satisfy them is also growing.

Reverting to a point made in Chapter 6, notice that an increasing number of services is being provided from without the farm and its farmstead. Electricity, water and sewerage are important examples but remember also the provision of articles like bread. Formerly, such articles or their equivalents were provided from internal resources or by an occasional excursion to market when large quantities would be bought for future use but now they come to the doorstep daily or weekly. The external relations of the farm are assuming an increasing importance.

Perhaps pride of place in these external contacts should be given to education. In an illiterate peasant society the offspring are pressed into work of all kinds at a tender age, whether it be to watch the livestock or fetch water. When educational facilities are provided, and especially when schooling is made compulsory, the young must leave home daily. When the dwellings are gathered together, no child need travel very far but where there are dispersed settlements considerable distances may be involved. In Britain, the local authority is obliged, if so required, to provide transport when the journey exceeds 3·2 kilometres and this is a very costly service in the remoter rural areas. Over much of the world, children customarily travel several kilometres each way daily on foot. Clearly, this provides a strong incentive to live in or near a village with a school, to ease the burden of daily travel imposed on the children and also the parents if they transport their offspring.

The matter does not rest there. The shortage of teachers throughout the world is very grave and therefore attempts are being made to derive the maximum benefit from the staff that is available. One manifestation of this policy is the attempt to close down the smaller rural schools all over Britain, bringing the children into larger units where they may be better grouped according to age and ability than is possible in the one- or two-teacher, all-age primary school. At the same time, the specialist skills of teachers are available to more pupils. Hence, the smaller villages are tending to lose their schools. Furthermore, where many parents are acutely conscious of the advantages conferred by a good education, there is a strong demand for a choice of facilities. A scantily peopled area cannot support more than one institution, so parents who are not satisfied with the local school must either face a long daily journey for their children, plus the possibility of considerable expense, or move house to a larger community.

Consequences

Manifold are the consequences of these developments. The most convenient approach is to discuss each major type of consequence arising from the interplay of all the considerations mentioned above. A reduction in the relative cost of movement within the farm means that when a farmer considers applying more labour, etc., to a distant field he has to reckon with a smaller cost on account of distance than formerly. The further away is the field, the greater will the proportionate saving be. That this will be so is evident from the following example. Consider two separate plots of land, one adjacent to the farmstead and the other at some remove. The former incurs virtually no transport costs, the latter a great deal. Were the ease of movement to become so great that it cost nothing, being effortless and instantaneous, then the proportionate advantage to the further plot must be the greater.

Thus, any decline in the relative cost of transport within the farm will mean that the level of gross and net output obtained from the land will diminish with distance less rapidly than before. This means that it becomes possible to intensify production over a greater part of the holding and the zoning of types and intensities of production will become less evident. Where the holding is sufficiently small, or the diminution in transport costs is adequately big, then zoning within the farm arising from the distance factor may well disappear. This will happen because the relative advantages of location become so small as hardly to matter, being outweighed by other considerations.

The point is admirably illustrated by the adoption of aerial techniques in the sheep-grazing areas of South Island, New Zealand. Holdings here are often many hundreds, even thousands, of hectares in extent, frequently running up from the accessible plateaux to the broken lower mountain slopes. By aerial seeding and fertilizing and the dropping of fencing supplies, it has been possible to extend the area of intensive grazing into the formerly inaccessible parts of the holdings, helping substantially to increase wool and meat production. On a less spectacular scale, the same process operates widely over the world and is one factor among many leading to an increase in agricultural supplies and a raising of rural living standards. The converse of this proposition is that, along with many other factors, it is possible for a given labour force, say a family, to cultivate a larger area than formerly. Or, in cultivating a given size of farm, a family can now dispense with hired labour. These latter aspects of the matter are more relevant for commercial, non-peasant economies where there are alternative occupations outside agriculture than they are for over-populated peasant countries like China and India with a high level of rural un- and under-employment. In England and Wales, there is a tendency for farms to become larger, though only slowly. Between 1913 and 1966, the proportion of the farm area in holdings under 8 hectares fell from 5·7 to 3·4 per cent in England and 9·1 to 5·4 per cent in Wales.[4] At the same time, the proportion of land in the larger farms rose somewhat. Altogether more important has been the exodus of wage labour from the land, while the number of farmers (owners and tenants) has remained roughly

TABLE 23[5]

ENGLAND AND WALES, 1851–1951:
PERSONS OCCUPIED IN AGRICULTURE
(*Thousands*)

Year	Farmers	Relatives occupied on the farm	Contract workers on the farm	Others in agriculture	Total in agriculture
1851	249	112	1,268	79	1,708
1911	229	115	688	155	1,186*
1931	248	81	539	131	999
1951	263	88	483	132	966

* Differs from the sum of the parts owing to rounding.

constant (Table 23). This table cannot be continued to 1961 owing to a change in classification for that year but the total agricultural labour force in England and Wales had by then fallen to 508,000 and it appears that within this over-all decline there has been a slight fall in the category 'farmers'. These trends do not arise solely from the considerations mentioned above, but nevertheless the diminution in the costs of transport within farms has contributed to the increase in farm size and exodus of rural labour.

An interesting, but minor, further consequence of this ability to intensify production up to the periphery of the holding relates to land consolidation. In preparing a scheme, it is normal for a survey to be carried out to establish the value of each parcel of land and so of each entire holding. On this basis, the new holdings are planned so that the farmers receive holdings which bear the same proportion to the new total value of farm land as the old ones did to the previous aggregate. In some cases, it may be necessary to make a cash adjustment where exact equity cannot otherwise be maintained. From the analysis which has been developed, it is quite evident that two adjacent parcels of lands may be identical in every particular of natural endowment but, being situated on different farms at different distances from the farmsteads, have markedly different values to their owners. In the process of reallocation, they may well be given to some third person and their space-relationships with the new farmstead will differ from what they previously were. Clearly, it is a very tricky matter to make an accurate allowance for these changes in value, and in practice the matter appears to be very largely neglected. In so far as the technical changes which have been mentioned are applied, with a consequent general intensification of farming on the further plots, by so much is this problem of equity less important and the more justifiable it is to ignore the matter. Exactly the same argument applies to the assessment of land taxes.

It is becoming increasingly possible for the dwelling to be removed from the territory which is cultivated and in many respects such separation is becoming more desirable. One manifestation of this has already been noted; in the recent Dutch reclamation schemes, houses for wage workers are frequently built in the villages instead of adjacent to the farmstead. A similar movement is occurring in Britain, because of the increasing difficulty that owners have in letting to agricultural workers cottages which are isolated and hard to reach. Many of these, especially in southern England, are being taken over as weekend cottages by urban dwellers seeking to escape from bricks and mortar. To an increasing extent, agricultural wage workers live in villages and hamlets instead of dispersed dwellings.

Much more extreme examples are reported from the United States, where two graphic but rather odd terms have come into use: 'suitcase' and 'sidewalk' farmers. The former are defined as persons who live more than 48 kilometres from the border of the county in which the land they cultivate lies. Frequently, such persons lead a migratory kind of existence, following the seasons northward at ploughing, planting and harvesting times, thereby providing extended use for the equipment they own. 'Sidewalk' farmers are those who live in nucleated settlements, cultivating land that may be some kilometres away. The importance of these farming categories in some parts of the United States is shown by the following figures:

TABLE 24[6]

UNITED STATES: 'SUITCASE' AND 'SIDEWALK' FARMING
IN THREE COUNTIES
(*Percentage of Operators*)

	Sully County, South Dakota 1950	Traill County, North Dakota 1953	Toole County, Montana 1955
Dispersed farmsteads	81·0	85·9	67·6
'Sidewalk'	8·5	14·1	29·7
'Suitcase'	10·5	—	2·7
	100·0	100·0	100·0

These are areas in which much grain is grown. It is interesting to observe that both 'suitcase' and 'sidewalk' farmers tend to emphasize cereals, notably wheat, more than do the farmers residing on their properties, at the same time growing less animal fodder. Despite the improvement of communications, some response to distance is called for, affecting the nature of the agriculture.

Where animals form an important feature of the economy, the possibilities for this type of change in residential location are somewhat limited. However, another contemporary development with important potential repercussions for the future is the growing interest in the efficiency with which birds and animals convert feeds into useful products—eggs, meat or milk. Such efficiency is achieved partly through careful breeding and partly by strictly controlled ingestion. Such control may preclude free ranging and often requires the animals or birds to be closely confined, all feed being brought to them. 'Broiler' chickens are an important case in point, but pigs are so treated and to an increasing extent veal calves and beef cattle are being reared by these methods. An interesting sidelight on this question is provided by test cases that were heard in the late 1950s and early 1960s in the United Kingdom, to establish whether the buildings in which these livestock are reared should be rated as industrial or agricultural hereditaments: though they continue to rate as agricultural, it is significant that the matter should have been raised in the courts. The conjunction of these new production techniques in animal husbandry and the transport improvements already noted indicates that it is becoming increasingly possible to separate the land from the dwellings and associated livestock facilities.

Great efforts have been directed towards the breeding of animals, principally cattle, capable of withstanding extreme conditions of heat. There has been considerable success but one of the limiting factors is the provision of adequate fodder in tropical regions. Good breeding in the absence of good feeding is a waste of time. It appears that in the tropical and equatorial parts of the world adequate fodder can be best provided by special crops rather than improved ranges and this argues the advantages of stall-feeding in many cases. This is especially so in areas of intensive arable farming where much of the feed for livestock is the waste or residue of crops used in other ways. There is the further advantage with stall-feeding that the climatic environment of the beasts can be controlled to a greater or lesser extent. It may not be altogether fanciful to imagine that it will be more profitable to breed for high efficiency in the conversion of feed and to provide air-conditioning than to breed for high resistance to adverse climatic conditions. After all, the design of modern chicken houses and pig pens is, among other things, an exercise in the economical control of temperature, humidity and ventilation.[7]

With irrigation, the problem is much less tractable. Only with the development of remote-controlled techniques for regulating the water supplies would it be possible for farmers to live away from their holdings. Since irrigated areas are commonly ones supporting a dense population, social intercourse and the provision of services are relatively easy even for dispersed settlements. Hence the advantages of nucleation are much less apparent in this case.

Clearly, with the important exception of irrigation farming, there is a tendency which we may expect to continue for agricultural settlements to become increasingly nucleated or, in the terminology of location studies, agglomerated. At first sight, this appears to contradict the conclusion reached in Chapter 4 that a spontaneous dispersal is occurring widely over the world. The apparent discrepancy may be reconciled in the following way. First, that which is currently happening in a country such as the United Kingdom or United States—agglomeration—may not yet be appropriate for much poorer nations but is likely to become so with the passage of time. Second, where there has been an excessive concentration of the rural population into a few enormous settlements, some degree of dispersal is requisite if the farming is to be improved. The question really turns on the extent to which dispersal should take place; it would appear that in some cases placing the farmsteads on the holdings is going too far.

Here lies an acute problem in planning the layout of new settlements. Where the existing peasantry is poor, illiterate and unskilled in intensive forms of agriculture and lacks mechanical equipment, it is without question essential to locate the farmsteads on the holdings. But this lays the foundations for an increase in wealth, better standards of education, more leisure, all forces which are likely to create conditions in which there is a growing desire to locate the dwellings in nucleated groups, a more pressing economic need to do so, and a greater ability to act upon these pressures. Should the layout conform to the initial needs, or the prospective ones? Or is a later change in the settlement pattern to be tolerated? Or what compromise solution should be adopted?

It is impossible to give a definitive answer to these questions. However, since it appears that the long-term trend is towards concentration of the rural populace, it is justifiable to argue that in any scheme for agricultural settlement the dwellings should be brought together into groups or villages to the maximum extent that, in the light of particular circumstances, can be tolerated. In this way, the longer-term problems of adjustment may be minimized and the maximum concession is made to a feeling common among persons accustomed to living in nucleated settlements, that they do not at first like the loneliness of living in dispersed dwellings.

Last among the consequences to be noted at the small scale but by no means the least important is that, in so far as the distribution of production within the farm is less dependent upon location with respect to the farmstead, it must become relatively more affected by other factors. In practice, these are the conditions of the natural environment. To an increasing extent, crops can be grown on the land which is best suited to give a high yield of good quality, yet another factor working towards an increase in yields and a general improvement in the productivity of both land and labour. This argument will be developed more fully in the context of the larger scales, the region and the world, and all that is here necessary is to note that a phenomenon which is chiefly significant at the larger scale is also apparent at the smaller.

Cheaper transport

Let us, then, turn to the wider view and look first at the cheapening of transport. There are three major ways in which transport costs have become and are becoming less in relation to the value of goods:

(1) The substitution of improved means of transport for more rudimentary methods.

(2) Improvements within individual transport media.

(3) The greater degree of processing undergone by products and changes in the type of product towards the more valuable ones.

In the next few paragraphs each will be examined in turn.

The spread of new transport techniques—whether stagecoach, canal, railway, motor vehicles, steam and diesel ships or aeroplanes—yields savings in transport costs which are sufficiently great and widespread to be obvious. There is no need to argue the case and it will suffice to give one or two illustrations to show how great the savings may be. De Foville,[8] writing in 1880, quoted the following approximate figures in French francs per metric-ton kilometre:

	Francs	*Cents*
Porter	3	33
Muleteer	—	87
Camel caravan	—	48
Carriages, 17th-century, at 1880 prices	1	50
Carriages, 19th-century	—	20
Railways, early 19th-century	—	25
Railways, 1870's	—	6

A modern example comes from Kenya, where porters or donkeys carried goods in the northern coastal belt at $1·0–$1·75 per ton mile. With the opening of a road in 1953, motor trucks handled this traffic at between 50 and 75 cents per ton mile.[9] Wherever the existing level of economic development is low, there is plenty of scope for benefits of these magnitudes to be obtained and—as argued earlier—

it appears that production expenses do not fall by so much and so quickly. Hence, the process of substituting media of transport leads to a reduction in the cost of transport in relation to the value of the commodities carried.

When it comes to changes within a single medium of transport, the problem of measurement becomes acute. There are several reasons for this. First, it is not always possible to obtain the relevant figures. Second, money values change and the longer the period considered the greater is the difficulty of making the appropriate adjustments. Third, the quality of the service alters—its speed and reliability, for example. The other two factors relate to the characteristics of the traffic. Even if the actual operating costs remain constant, the average cost per metric-ton kilometre will vary either if the length of haul changes or if the composition of the traffic alters. In the first case, the fixed terminal expenses are spread over a differing length of journey. In the second, each commodity has its own unique combination of characteristics and consequently individual cost of handling. For these reasons, the most reliable measure of changes in transport costs would be by comparisons of rates on specified goods between stated points, related to the value of the commodities. Adequate data of this kind are not available and we must be content with less satisfactory materials which should be interpreted with caution.

For the purpose, the best-documented medium of transport is ocean shipping, for which reasonably good records of freight rates go back into the middle of the last century. On the basis of such records, it is possible to construct index numbers showing the general level of freights in any one year compared with a selected base year. During the last quarter of the nineteenth century and the first decade of the twentieth, freight rates fell spectacularly from index 175 in 1876–80 to 100 in the base year 1913. Since then, there has been a considerable increase in rates, largely on account of world-wide inflation. To allow for these variations in money values, it is possible to compare the index of freight rates with an index of the prices of goods entering international trade. If the former is divided by the latter, an index of 'real' freights is obtained; the higher the index number, the higher the cost of shipping in relation to the value of the goods carried. This index of 'real' freights shows a fall from 172 in 1876–80 to 100 in 1913, which is almost identical to the decline in actual freight rates. This is due to the stability of prices in this period. By 1951–5, the index had fallen to 76, owing to the rise in price of commodities being much greater than the rise in freight rates. Over a period of some eighty years, the 'real' cost of shipping has fallen by almost three-fifths.[10]

An indirect method of measuring trends in the relative cost of overland transport in the United States is provided by data on the productivity of the various sectors of the economy. Using output in relation to the total factor input, Mansfield[11] obtained the results shown in Table 25. It is quite evident that over a long span of years productivity increases have been considerably greater in the transport industries than in the economy as a whole and it is a reasonable inference that therefore transport is becoming cheaper relative to most goods and services.

TABLE 25

UNITED STATES: AVERAGE ANNUAL RATES OF CHANGE IN OUTPUT
PER UNIT FACTOR INPUT IN TRANSPORT AND THE
NATIONAL ECONOMY, 1890–1953

	Average annual per cent increase
National economy	1·7
All transport	3·1
Railways	2·6

A third piece of evidence comes from New Zealand and relates to revenues for goods traffic on the railways. This country possesses records which make possible an analysis extending over a much longer period of time than is generally the case. In the years 1884–6, a revenue of 2·12d. was obtained for each metric-ton kilometre of goods traffic and thereafter there was a continuous fall to 1·48d. in the period 1927–31. These revenues have been converted to 1939 prices and therefore show a substantial decline in the relative cost of transport in this period. Since the Depression, the level of 'real' freights has oscillated round roughly the same level, tending to rise somewhat in the 1950's (being 1·61d. per metric-ton kilometre in 1952–6) but falling back to 1·40d. in the period 1961–5. This represents a fall in the relative cost of rail transport of roughly one-quarter in the period covered.[12] Examination of the patchy evidence available indicates that a change in traffic composition is not the cause of this decline. On the other hand, there has been a notable increase in the average length of haul and in traffic density, both potent factors for lower costs. It is more important to observe that whereas the railways were making a substantial profit before the First World War, shortly afterwards profits began to decline, and today losses are being incurred. Thus, the costs shown above represent costs to the users, not the cost of providing the service. This does not destroy the value of the figures, for we are interested to know those costs which enter into individual decisions, affecting location and production choices. The revenues obtained are won in competition with other media of transport, even though in New Zealand legislation restricts this competition quite severely in favour of the railways. The fact that the 'real' costs on the railways have not risen since the First World War proves that the other media of transport have, at the very least, not become relatively more expensive. Since there has been a considerable transfer of traffic to road vehicles, it seems reasonable to infer that, in fact, road transport has been getting relatively cheaper.

The three pieces of evidence offered above find confirmation in statements such as that of Lord Douglas of Kirtleside, that in the period 1927–57 'the cost per seat-mile of the transport aeroplane has been reduced by more than 75 per cent'.[13] It appears safe to conclude that there has been a substantial decline in 'real' transport costs in the last few decades. The moot point is whether this decline can be expected to continue into the future. This is indeed a difficult problem. In part, it will depend upon the rate at which technical innovation proceeds in the transport industries and in the economy generally; this it is impossible to forecast. On the other hand, it is readily apparent that the application of known engineering techniques could cause some big cost reductions at the regional scale, even where modern transport facilities already exist. A recent example is the opening of the St Lawrence Seaway in 1959, which has reduced freight rates to the interior littoral of north America to a marked degree. The more recently completed road tunnel under Mont Blanc, connecting France and Italy, provides the first all-season road connection over the Alps between the two nations. The projected tunnel between England and France would yield a big saving in time and probably also in cost. Other examples which come to mind are the lakes formed behind the Kariba Dam and on the Volta river; both provide many tens of kilometres of navigable water.

The third manner in which transport costs are declining in relative importance arises from the changing nature of agricultural produce. As living standards rise, dietary habits change, leading to an increase in the relative importance of foods like meat, dairy produce, fruit and vegetables, which tend to replace the staple foodstuffs of grains and tubers. These higher-class foods are more difficult to transport than are crops like wheat, being more perishable; but their much higher value in relation to bulk means that relatively speaking the cost of transport is lower. To the extent that dietary habits continue to change in the direction which has so far been apparent in the more advanced countries, there will be a decline in the significance of transport in agriculture. Second, and working in the same direction, is the increasing extent to which foodstuffs are processed. This may take the simple form of washing potatoes or carrots on the farm prior to dispatch to market, or it may be the growing popularity of pre-cooked and frozen foods. In such cases, the value of the commodity is raised without adding materially to transport costs.

Consequences

The most obvious consequence of lower 'real' transport costs is a widening of the zone of supply of agricultural products, as exemplified in the case of dairy and horticultural foods in the United Kingdom (see Chapter 5). In itself this is obvious and commonplace but it is worth pausing to notice one consequence. Particularly when these transport improvements are related to the astonishing increase of urban populations in some countries, the shifts in supply zones may be very rapid indeed. In principle, what happens is that each supply zone tends to expand, so that any individual product is obtained at a greater remove than formerly from the main areas of urban agglomeration. In this way, any particular piece of land may be put to a succession of different uses within a relatively short time. The tendency will be for these uses to become progressively more intensive, as the zones of intensive production near the urban concentrations expand, replacing the more extensive forms of cultivation at the greater distances. The margin of cultivation is thereby extended.

This point is well made by Schlebecker,[14] who was concerned to provide a theoretical framework for the study of agricultural history and showed that von Thünen's ideas do have a real relevance. He drew attention to two main points. First, that in past centuries there were many urban concentrations which were relatively small, each with its own zones of agricultural production, whereas in the present day there are far fewer, but each much bigger and influencing a great part of the world. Indeed, he suggested that western Europe and the eastern United States may be regarded as one metropolitan area in the context of the world. Second, and closely related to the first, he noticed the sequence of land uses which may be experienced by any one area, observing the manner in which they repeat the order of intensity of farming types. In America, he said: 'On a single farm a man might in his own lifetime be in cattle country, wheat country, corn country, and dairy country.' The moving frontier and the attendant changes in land use can only be fully understood in terms of location principles, which provide a necessary framework for analysis.

A closely related phenomenon is that of an increase in the degree of regional specialization. This arises in the following manner. With a decline in transport costs, the advantage conferred by proximity to markets and to inputs diminishes in absolute importance. Consequently, other location factors must assume a larger relative significance, principally conditions of climate, soil and topography. Collectively, these have a big effect upon the earliness of the crop season and thus on the price which can be obtained for the produce and on the costs of production. The consequence is that instead of a particular crop being grown near the consuming centres and necessarily under very diverse physical conditions, it is increasingly possible for it to be grown in a limited number of places which physically are well suited to its requirements. The advantages of lower production costs and/or earlier season are not fully absorbed by transport costs, as previously they were. An example is provided by the British glasshouse industry, which, on one calculation, could make a net saving of over £2 million annually were all glasshouses to be located in the climatically most favourable southern parts of the country.[15]

Baker discussed the matter at some length as long ago as 1921,[16] drawing attention to the influence of topography, soil fertility, moisture and temperature. What Baker called regional 'specialization' of production may also be termed regional 'agglomeration' of enterprises, for if production is locally concentrated so also must producers be congegated together. The agglomeration of like enterprises at the regional level may be compared with the agglomeration of dwellings into nucleated settlements discussed earlier in this chapter—a similar phenomenon but affecting a different element of the agricultural economy.

Several other factors are working in the same direction, encouraging local specialization of production but differing in importance from product to product. One of the outstanding developments in the retailing trade of fresh food in the United Kingdom since the last war, following the lead of the United States, has been the expansion of business handled by big chain stores, such as Marks & Spencer. Organizations of this kind require large quantities of standardized produce. But graded and branded goods are of increasing importance in the trade of other shops, notably the self-service establishments. This development demands either that production be on a large scale or that the output of numerous small holdings should pass through a single grading and packing centre, such as a co-operative. In the latter case, there are self-evident advantages in having a number of producers close together, especially if the central organization also supplies farming requisites. The establishment of Home Grown Fruits, Ltd, in 1961, to grade and market between one-quarter and one-third of the commercial apple crop in Britain produced by only 300 growers[17] is a recent example that provides some parallels with the earlier evolution of hop production and marketing in Kent.[18] Since there seems to be every likelihood that standardized, branded produce will take an increasing share of the market, there will be a continuing pressure towards local specialization.

Closely related to the above is the ability of large organizations to bargain for favourable transport rates. One of the classic cases is that of California in the United States; this state managed to establish itself early as the major supplier of the east coast for many types of fruit and vegetable and, because of the large scale of shipments, was able to obtain favourable treatment from the railways. Florida found it difficult to break into this market, having initially a low level of production and therefore being unable to get such good freight rates. Road transport has given Florida its chance because there appear to be few economies of scale in road transport operations[19] and consequently the small scale of production in the beginning was much less of a handicap.

Third, production techniques in all types of agricultural enterprise are getting more and more elaborate, requiring a greater degree of technical knowledge and skill. It is more difficult for each farmer to keep abreast of developments, even if he has the ability and the interest to follow events closely. Increasingly do farmers have to rely upon outside guidance and advice, whether this be provided by the official National Agricultural Advisory Service or firms selling agricultural necessities. With specialist types of production, which are becoming more and more important, specialized information is needed, and this can be and is most effectively provided where particular types of enterprise are locally concentrated. Elsewhere, the standard of service is inevitably poorer. An example of the increasing complexity of farming, even for staple products, is provided by a new selective weedkiller known as barbane and effective against the troublesome wild oat in corn crops. It has been discovered that this substance must not be used on winter wheat in the month of March, though spraying both before and after leaves the wheat crop unharmed. Certain varieties of barley are as susceptible as wild oats while others are immune. The reasons for these curious effects are not yet known.[20] It is becoming increasingly common for the smaller producers to hire the services of contracting firms or the use of particular pieces of machinery. When the equipment is specialized, it is evidently going to be easier and cheaper to arrange such services where there is a reasonable demand which will keep the machinery in use than where the demand is sporadic and small.

A fifth factor of importance is the growing scale of factory manufacturing and processing operations. The rapidity of this growth in factory size can be seen from Table 26, which relates to persons employed in the United Kingdom. Textiles have been excluded because they are a major declining industry, with a diminishing number of persons employed in each factory. The rate of growth in average size of establishment is greater than is indicated, owing to the falling proportion of employees engaged in small factories with 10 employees or fewer; 12 per cent in 1924 and only 4 per cent in 1954. Since the productivity of labour has been rising, the size of factories as measured by output has been increasing even more rapidly than is indicated by the employment data. Hence, the processing of agricultural products is being done in increasingly large units—all over the world—and this encourages a larger output in the area around a factory. This is especially important where the raw product is highly perishable, like tea, is very bulky and loses much weight in processing, as in the case of butter and cheese, or yields a waste product which is returned to many of the farms, for example, the pulp yielded by sugar beet. These characteristics may be present in various combinations. Since there is every prospect that technical development will produce further scale economies in processing, there will be a continuing tendency for the output of particular items to be gathered round a limited number of factories.

TABLE 26

UNITED KINGDOM, 1924–61: AVERAGE NUMBER OF EMPLOYED PERSONS
PER MANUFACTURING ESTABLISHMENT;
TEXTILES AND MINING EXCLUDED

	1961	1954	1951	1948	1935	1935	1930	1924
All establishments employing over 10	149·0	133·6	126·6	122·3	102·3	97·5	88·4	87·5
Food, drink and tobacco	139·2	104·6	95·9	86·0	76·4	76·2	66·4	70·3

Source: Periodic censuses of production, published by the Board of Trade, and Annual Abstract of Statistics. There was a radical change of classification after 1935.

Reverting for a moment to the effects of a cheapening of transport in encouraging a greater degree of local specialization of production, there is a seeming paradox which warrants attention. Brinkmann[21] observed that in some areas a lowering of transport costs could lead to a diversification of the agricultural economy. The reasoning behind this conclusion is as follows. Imagine an area which is inherently capable of producing several products, but is so situated with respect to markets as to be at the extensive margin of cultivation, finding only one crop yields a sufficient return to be worth growing. Under these conditions, monoculture must necessarily occur. If 'real' transport costs become less, one or more of the enterprises which potentially could be engaged is brought within the ambit of possibilities. Under conditions of perfect adjustment, this might merely mean the replacement of one type of monoculture by another as the production zones expand. But since adjustment never is perfect, farmers will have the choice of two or more crops, differences in the profitability of which are too small to bother about. Mixed farming is then likely to occur. It is, however, probable, even if there are marked differences in the profitability of the individual products, that farmers will choose mixed cultivation for at least three reasons:

(1) The combination of products will probably mean a net increase in yields and hence in the net profit of the farm as a whole.

(2) If one crop fails in any year, another may survive or even be highly successful. This helps to increase the stability of the farm income.

(3) There is likely to be a better distribution of work throughout the year and therefore a more economical use of labour and machinery.

While an increasing degree of regional specialization is the general trend, this is quite compatible with some change towards diversification at the extensive margin of cultivation as it ceases to be the margin.

The evidence and arguments so far presented have all tended in one direction, to the conclusion that agglomeration is likely to become increasingly important. There is one important set of circumstances which appears to be working in the opposite direction. Schultz and Price[22] have observed that the payments which are made for the use of land, or rent, are becoming a smaller proportion of the expenses of agriculture in the more advanced countries. Price adduces two reasons for this: first, that agricultural production is being intensified generally; second, that there is a growing proportion of intensively farmed products, a shift from wheat to poultry, from potatoes to dairy produce. Both trends imply an increasing use of fertilizers, machinery, sprays, etc.: this means that the inherent qualities of the soil are becoming progressively less important for agricultural production. We would not, then, expect agglomeration of production into areas which are well suited physically.

Price omits to consider that some of the decline in the importance of rent arises from a third factor, that which we have been considering. With improved means of communication, the importance of location with respect to the market has diminished and this causes a reduction in the relative importance of rent.[23] Thus, the decline in the relative importance of land in the operations of agriculture attributable to the increasing use of other inputs is less than is suggested by Schultz and Price.

The second point to notice is that in most countries, or very large sections of them, the price which a farmer has to pay for manufactured inputs does not vary at all from place to place, or only very slightly. Manufacturers of machinery in particular tend to fix a uniform price throughout their sales area in a country and the same is true for most other requisites except the most bulky. Where regional price variations do occur, as between countries, they tend to be fairly small, because the cost of transport on manufactured goods is not proportionately very great. It therefore happens that whereas location has a very big effect upon the price which a farmer receives for his produce, it has a much lesser effect upon the costs of his inputs of machinery, fertilizers and buildings.[24] Reinforcing this contrast is the habit of many trades unions of bargaining for national wage levels; in the United Kingdom the agreed minimum rates of pay for agricultural workers are uniform throughout the country.

With changes in the cost structure of agriculture, especially towards the use of more equipment and fertilizer, there is a growing proportion of the total costs of production which are uninfluenced by location or are influenced to only a small extent. Thus, it is entirely compatible to argue that while the physical qualities of the land— soil, slope, climate etc.—are becoming less important in relation to all the factors influencing the profits of farming, nevertheless among those factors which vary in quality or price from one place to another the physical environment is assuming more significance. The physical environment is therefore playing a bigger part in determining the location of production.

The conclusion is inescapable. At all scales, in the economically more advanced nations, powerful economic forces are working for an increasing degree of agglomeration. This is not to say that these constraints are ineluctable; where, for a variety of reasons, such tendencies towards centralization and specialization are regarded as undesirable, action can be taken to redress the 'imbalance.' Such action will be motivated by social and political needs and it is entirely legitimate that these should have precedence over economic considerations. This is not the place to take up these wider issues. My purpose will have been achieved if such decisions are informed by a fuller understanding of the economic forces which operate to mould the geography of the world.

BIBLIOGRAPHICAL NOTES

1. M. Clawson, 'Factors and forces affecting the optimum rural settlement pattern in the United States', *Economic Geography*, 1966, pp. 283–93.

2. U. Sorbi, *Borgo a Mozzano*, 1955, p. 48.

3. *Agricultural Aviation*, Vol. I, no. 2, 1959, p. 31 and *The Times*, 20 February 1967. See also 'Aircraft in agriculture', in *Power to Produce*, United States Department of Agriculture Yearbook, 1960.

4. G. P. Hirsch, 'The size of farm holdings in England and Wales', *Farm Economist*, 1958, p. 84, and Ministry of Agriculture, *Agricultural Statistics*. A slight change in classification has the effect that the decline of small farms is understated.

5. J. R. Bellerby, 'The distribution of manpower in agriculture and industry 1851–1951', *Farm Economist*, 1958, p. 3.

6. W. M. Kollmorgen and G. F. Jenks, 'Suitcase farming in Sully County, South Dakota', 'Sidewalk farming in Toole County, Montana, and Trail County, North Dakota', *Annals*, Association of American Geographers, 1958, pp. 27–40 and 209–31.

7. 'Environment of animals', in *Power to Produce*, 1960, *supra*. For a survey of current practices and problems in the tropics, see G. Williamson and W. J. A. Payne, *An Introduction to Animal Husbandry in the Tropics*, 1959.

8. A. de Foville, *La Transformation des Moyens de Transport et ses Conséquences Économiques et Sociales*, 1880.

9. W. A. Hance, *African Economic Development*, 1958, p. 87.

10. Index of ocean freights from C. P. Kindleberger, 'Industrial Europe's terms of trade on current account, 1870–1953', *Economic Journal*, 1955, p. 23, supplemented from *The Economist*. Index of the prices of goods entering international trade from Mr D. T. Healey, Institute of Commonwealth Studies, Oxford.

11. E. Mansfield, 'Innovation and technical change in the railroad industry', p. 172, in National Bureau of Economic Research, *Transportation Economics*, 1965.

12. The tonnage and revenue figures are published in the official *Yearbook* and in the *Appendices* of the House of Representatives for the whole period. Data on length of haul and ton miles are also available from 1926–7 in the same sources. For earlier years, the ton miles were obtained by interpolating from data published for the years 1883–4 to 1894–5, *Appendix*, D–2, No. 8, 1895. The price index was taken from the *Yearbooks*, and extended back by data taken from J. W. McIllwraith, 'Price variations in New Zealand', *Economic Journal*, 1913, p. 348.

13. Lord Douglas of Kirtleside, 'The economics of speed', *Modern Transport*, 16 February 1957, p. 11.

14. J. T. Schlebecker, 'The world metropolis and the history of American agriculture', *Journal of Economic History*, 1960, pp. 187–208.

15. L. G. Bennett, 'Diminished competitive power of the British glasshouse industry because of mal-location', University of Reading, Department of Agricultural Economics, *Miscellaneous Studies*, No. 26, 1963. See also: Best and Gasson, 1966, *supra* (ch. 5).

16. O. E. Baker, 'The increasing importance of the physical conditions in determining the utilization of land for agricultural and forest production in the United States', *Annals*, Association of American Geographers, 1921, pp. 17–46.

17. *The Times*, 26 September 1963.

18. D. W. Harvey, 'Locational change in the Kentish hop industry and the analysis of land use patterns', *Transactions and Papers*, Institute of British Geographers, no. 33, 1963, pp. 123–44.

19. A. J. Harrison, 'Economies of scale and the structure of the road haulage industry', *Oxford Economic Papers*, 1963, pp. 287–307.

20. *The Times*, 14 November 1960.

21. Brinkmann, 1935, *supra* (ch. 2).

22. T. W. Schultz, 'The declining economic importance of agricultural land', *Economic Journal*, 1951, pp. 725–40; O. T. W. Price, 'The economic significance of land as a factor of production, with particular reference to agricultural land', *Farm Economist*, 1953, pp. 239–53.

23. M. Chisholm, 'Agricultural production, location and rent', *Oxford Economic Papers*, 1961, pp. 342–59.

24. M. Chisholm, *Geography and Economics*, 1966, ch. 7.

SELECT BIBLIOGRAPHY

Most of the works here listed appear in the Bibliographical Notes accompanying the various chapters. The list is intended solely as a guide to the more important works which may be used further to pursue points made in the text.

ALONSO, W.: *Location and Land Use: Toward a General Theory of Land Rent*, 1964.

BENEDICT, E. T. (Ed.): *Theodor Brinkmann's Economics of the Farm Business*, 1935.

BERESFORD, M. W., and ST JOSEPH, J. K.: *Medieval England: an Aerial Survey*, 1958.

DE LA BLACHE, P. V.: *Principles of Human Geography*, English edn., 1926.

CHAMBERS, J. D., and MINGAY, G. E.: *The Agricultural Revolution 1750–1880*, 1966.

CHISHOLM, M.: 'Agricultural production, location and rent', *Oxford Economic Papers*, 1961, pp. 342–59.

CHISHOLM, M.: *Geography and Economics*, 1966.

CHRISTALLER, W.: *Central Places in Southern Germany*, 1966. (Translation from the German by W. Baskin.)

CLAPHAM, J. H.: *An Economic History of Modern Britain*, Vols. I and II, 1926 and 1932.

COHEN, R. L.: *The Economics of Agriculture*, 1957.

DARBY, H. C. (Ed.): *Historical Geography of England before 1800*, 1936.

DOVRING, F.: *Land and Labour in Europe in The Twentieth Century*, 3rd edn., 1965.

DUMONT, R.: *Types of Rural Economy*, English edn., 1957.

DUNN, E. S.: *The Location of Agricultural Production*, 1954.

EAST, W. G.: *An Historical Geography of Europe*, 5th edn., 1966.

ELLIS, H.: *British Railway History*, 2 vols., 1954 and 1959.

ELY, R. T., and WEHRWEIN, G. S.: *Land Economics*, 1940.

DE FOVILLE, A.: *La Transformation des Moyens de Transport et ses Conséquences Économiques et Sociales*, 1880.

HAGGETT, P.: *Locational Analysis in Human Geography*, 1965.

HALL, P.: *von Thünen's Isolated State*, 1966.

HARVEY, D. W.: 'Theoretical concepts and the analysis of agricultural land-use patterns in geography,' *Annals*, Association of American Geographers, 1966, pp. 361–74.

HEADY, E. O.: *Economics of Agricultural Production and Resource Use*, 1952.

HOOVER, E. M.: *The Location of Economic Activity*, 1948.

HOSKINS, W. G.: *The Making of the English Landscape*, 1955.

ISARD, W.: *Location and Space Economy*, 1956.

JACKMAN, W. T.: *The Development of Transportation in Modern England*, 2 vols., 1916.

JACOBY, E. H.: *Land Consolidation in Europe*, International Institute for Land Reclamation and Improvement, 1959.

JONASSON, O.: 'Agricultural regions of Europe,' *Economic Geography*, 1925, pp. 277–314.

LENNARD, R.: *Rural England 1086–1135: a Study of Social and Agrarian Conditions*, 1959.

LÖSCH, A.: *The Economics of Location*, English edn., 1954.

MARTIN, A.: *Economics and Agriculture*, 1958.

MEYNIER, A.: *Les Paysages Agraires*, 1958.

MURRAY, W. G.: *Farm Appraisal*, 2nd edn., 1950.

OHLIN, B.: *Interregional and International Trade*, 1933.

ORWIN, C. S., and ORWIN, C. S.: *The Open Fields*, 2nd edn., 1954.

PONSARD, C.: *Économie et Espace*, 1955; *History of Economic Location Theory*, English edn., 1967.

RUILLÈRE, G.: *Localisations et Rhythmes de l'Activité Agricole*, 1956.

SAUTTER, G.: 'A propos de quelques terroirs d'Afrique occidentale: essai comparatif', *Études rurales*, 1962, pp. 24–86.

SCHLEBECKER, J. T.: 'The world metropolis and the history of American agriculture', *Journal of Economic History*, 1960, pp. 187–208.

DE SCHLIPPÉ, P.: *Shifting Cultivation in Africa: the Zande System of Agriculture*, 1956.

SINCLAIR, R.: 'Von Thünen and urban sprawl', *Annals*, Association of American Geographers, 1967, pp. 72–87.

STAMP, L. D.: *The Land of Britain: its Use and Misuse*, 1948.

TAKES, H. P.: *Physical Planning in Connection with Land Reclamation and Improvement*, International Institute for Land Reclamation and Improvement, 1958.

TCHERKINSKY, M. N.: *L'Organisation Scientifique du Travail Agricole en Europe*, 1931.

VON THÜNEN, J. H.: see Hall, P.

WALD, H. P.: *Taxation of Agricultural Lands in Underdeveloped Economies*, 1959.

WARNTZ, W.: *Toward a Geography of Price*, 1959.

WEBER, A.: *Theory of the Location of Industries*, English edn., 1957.

WELLINGTON, A. M.: *The Economic Theory of the Location of Railways*, 6th edn., 1898.

WHETHAM, E. H.: *The Economic Background to Agricultural Policy*, 1960.

ZIPF, G. K.: *Human Behaviour and the Principle of Least Effort*, 1949.

INDEX